INSTRUCTIONS

FOR THE

SWORD, CARBINE, PISTOL, AND LANCE EXERCISE.

TOGETHER WITH

STANDING GUN DRILL,

FOR THE USE OF THE CAVALRY.

REVISED EDITION.

ADJUTANT GENERAL'S OFFICE, HORSE GUARDS,

1st JULY, 1858.

The Naval & Military Press Ltd

Published by the
The Naval & Military Press

in association with the Royal Armouries

Unit 10 Ridgewood Industrial Park,
Uckfield, East Sussex, TN22 5QE
Tel: +44 (0) 1825 749494
Fax: +44 (0) 1825 765701

MILITARY HISTORY AT YOUR FINGERTIPS
www.naval-military-press.com

ONLINE GENEALOGY RESEARCH
www.military-genealogy.com

ONLINE MILITARY CARTOGRAPHY
www.militarymaproom.com

The Library & Archives Department at the Royal Armouries Museum, Leeds, specialises in the history and development of armour and weapons from earliest times to the present day. Material relating to the development of artillery and modern fortifications is held at the Royal Armouries Museum, Fort Nelson.

For further information contact:
Royal Armouries Museum, Library, Armouries Drive,
Leeds, West Yorkshire LS10 1LT
Royal Armouries, Library, Fort Nelson, Down End Road, Fareham PO17 6AN

Or visit the Museum's website at
www.armouries.org.uk

In reprinting in facsimile from the original, any imperfections are inevitably reproduced and the quality may fall short of modern type and cartographic standards.

Printed and bound by CPI Antony Rowe, Eastbourne

CONTENTS.

SWORD EXERCISE.

CARBINE EXERCISE.

PISTOL EXERCISE

LANCE EXERCISE.

CONTENTS.

STANDING GUN DRILL.

GENERAL ORDER.

HORSE GUARDS,
1st *July*, 1858.

The following Rules and Regulations for the various Exercises laid down in this book having been approved, are to be observed and practised by the several Cavalry Regiments in Her Majesty's Service.

By Command of
His Royal Highness the Duke of Cambridge,
General Commanding-in-Chief,

G. A. WETHERALL,
Adjutant General.

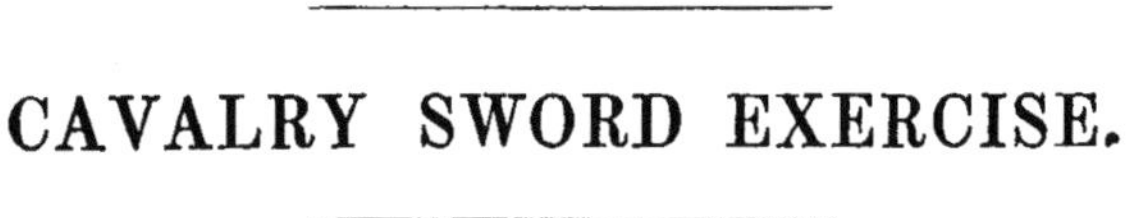

CAVALRY SWORD EXERCISE.

CAVALRY SWORD EXERCISE.

Introductory Remarks.

The following Instructions are progressively laid down as the surest and quickest mode of forming Swordsmen ; and the Drill Officers are to understand clearly, that when Recruits have completed their Preparatory and Drill Practices, *without* and *with* the sword, they need no longer be required to remember the precise order in which they are here given ; nor to repeat them, if sufficiently competent to go through the Review Exercises effectively, where every Cut, Point, and Guard, is shewn ; and the Swordsman ought to be made so perfect in each, as to be able to give any one separately, or such of them combined, as the Drill Officer may require.

Section I.

EXTENSION MOTIONS.

THESE motions tend to expand the chest, raise the head, throw back the shoulders, and strengthen the muscles of the back.

The squad being at "Attention," the caution is given :

First Extension Motions.

One—Bring the hand, arms, and shoulders to the front, the fingers lightly touching at the points, and the nails downwards; then raise them in a circular direction well above the head, the ends of the fingers still touching, the thumbs pointing to the rear, the elbows pressed back, and shoulders kept down.

Two—Separate and extend the arms and fingers upwards, forcing them obliquely back, until they come extended on a line with the shoulders ; and as they fall gradually from thence to the original position of "Attention," endeavour, as much as possible, to elevate the neck and chest.

Three—Turn the palms of the hands to the front, and press back the thumbs with the arms extended, and raise them to the rear until they meet above the head ; the fingers pointing upwards, and the thumbs locked with the left in front.

Four—Keep the knees and arms straight, and bend over until the hands touch the feet, the head being brought down in the same direction, and resume the " Third Motion," by raising the arms to the front.

Five—Resume the position of "Attention," as directed in " Second Motion."

The whole of these motions should be done very gradually, so as to feel the exertion of the muscles throughout, and the " First" and " Second" occasionally practised with the head turned, as much as possible, to the right or left ; and all the motions may be performed also, without any pause or separate word of command, so that they may lead into each other, the order in which they occur being occasionally varied.

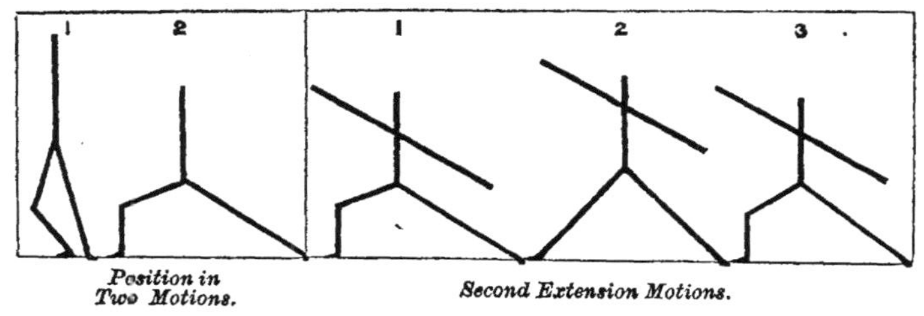

1
2
Position in
Two Motions.
1
2
3
Second Extension Motions.

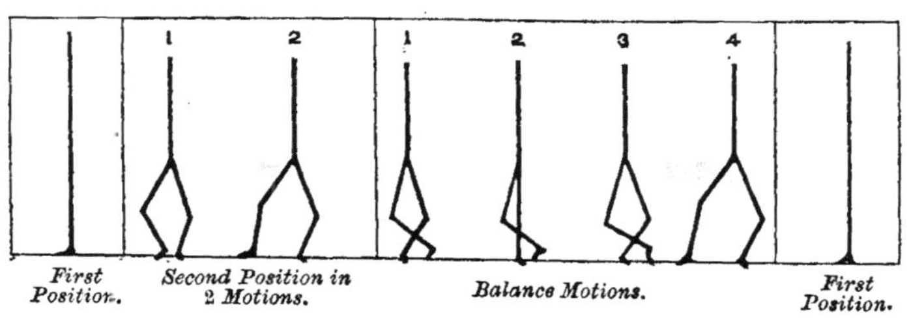

First
Position.
1
2
Second Position in
2 Motions.
1
2
3
4
Balance Motions.
First
Position.

First Position in Three Motions.

One—Move the hands smartly to the rear, the left grasping the right arm just above the elbow, and the right supporting the left arm under the elbow.

Two—Half face to the left, turning on the heels, so that the back of the left touches the inside of the right heel, the head retaining its position to the front.

Three—Bring the right heel before the left, the feet at right angles, the right foot pointing to the front, and the weight of the body resting on the left leg.

Second Position in Two Motions.

One—Bend the knees gradually, keeping them as much apart as possible, without raising the heels, or changing the erect position of the body.

Two—Step out smartly with the right foot about eighteen inches, in line with the left heel, the weight of the body remaining on the left leg, the right knee easy and flexible.

Balance Motions.

One—Move the right foot about eight inches to the rear of the left heel, the toe lightly touching the ground, with the heel perpendicular to it, keeping the knees well apart.

Two—Raise the body gradually by the extension of the left leg.

Three—Bend the left knee, resuming the position made previous to the " Second Motion."

Four—Advance the right leg, give a smart beat with the foot, and resume the " Second Position," from which " Balance Motions" commenced.

First Position—Extending both knees, bring the right heel back to the left.

Third Position in Two Motions.

One—Incline the right side to the front, so that the shoulder and knee are perpendicular to the point of the foot, keeping the body erect.

Two—Step out smartly to the front, about thirty-six inches, the knee perpendicular to the instep ; the left knee and foot kept straight and firm, the heels in a line, the body upright, and the shoulders square to the left.

Second Extension Motions.

One—Bring the arms to the front of the body, with the hands closed and the knuckles uppermost, touching each other below the lower button of the jacket ; raise them gradually until the wrists, by bearing inwards, touch the breast, the elbows being kept up ; then, by forcing back the shoulders, the hands will be drawn apart, and the motion is completed by sinking the elbows, and smartly extending the arms and fingers in a diagonal line, with the right wrist as high as the head, the shoulders kept down, and the thumbs inclined to the right.

For beginners, this motion may be divided,—by giving the word *Prepare* for the first part, and remaining perfectly steady, when the hands are brought to the breast, ready to separate ; then give the word *One* for the motion to be completed.

Two—Raise the body by extending the right leg.

Three—Bend the right knee, and advance the body so as to resume the "First Motion."

First Position—Spring up with the arms to the rear, and the right heel close to the left, which forms the "First Position," as before described.

Front—Come smartly to the position of "Attention ;" bringing the hands and feet, in one motion, to their proper places.

In the foregoing Instructions, the Positions and Movements, preparatory to using the sword, have been explained, giving a separate word of command for each motion respectively. The same positions must now be gone through, naming only (in the word of command) the position required, in order to practise the Recruit in changing the positions readily, without losing his balance, and in quick time,—distinguishing them by the word of command, *First, Second,* and *Third.*

Positions.

First—Raising the arms to the rear, and the right heel to the front, come at once to the "First Position."

Second—Come to "Second Position."

First	„	"First Position."
Third	„	"Third Position."
First	„	"First Position."
Second	„	"Second Position."
Third	„	"Third Position."
Second	„	"Second Position."

Single Attack—Raise the right foot and beat it smartly on the ground.

Double Attack—Raise the right foot as before, and beat it twice on the ground—first with the heel, then with the flat of the foot.

Advance—Move forward the right foot about six inches, and place it smartly on the ground ; then bring up the left foot lightly about the same distance.

Single Attack—As before.

Retire—Move the left foot lightly to the rear about six inches, the weight and balance of the body being, and continuing to rest, upon it ; then move the right foot back the same distance, and place it smartly on the ground.

Double Attack—As before.

Front—Resume position of " Attention."

The object of the preceding Positions and Movements is to give a free and active use of the limbs preparatory to using the sword.

The Instructor should prove the firmness of the position by bearing equally and firmly upon the shoulders of the Recruit during the changes in forming the "Positions" and " Balance Motions ;" by taking hold of his right wrist with both hands, (when in the " First " of the " Second Extension Motions ") and bearing upon it, in the direction of the left leg, upon the line of which the right arm should be, if properly placed : and making him also in each position move the fore part of the right foot up and down, without its motion affecting the body, which must be generally balanced, and rest upon the left leg, thereby giving greater flexibility to the right leg in moving forward to gain distance upon an adversary—or *vice versâ*, in retiring from his reach. No precise length can be assigned in moving the right leg to the front in the " Third Position," as it depends upon the length and stride of the person ; but it should not be beyond what may allow of his returning to the " First " or " Second Position " with quickness and perfect facility to himself.

When this section is practised as a drill for the limbs only, it should be performed with the left shoulder and left foot to the front, as well as with the right.

Section II.

SWORD EXERCISE.

Cuts—Guards—Points.

The Recruit being perfectly instructed in the preparatory movements, should now be given a sword and made acquainted with the strong and weak parts of it ; the " Fort " (strong) being the half of the blade near the hilt, the " Feeble " (weak) the half towards the point ; indeed, a knowledge of these distinctions is very material either in giving or guarding a Cut, as much depends upon their proper application. From the hilt upwards, in opposing the blade of an adversary, the strength of the defence decreases in proportion as the Cut is received towards the point ; and, *vice versâ*, it increases from the point downwards. The same grasp of the Sword is to be retained throughout the exercise, to ensure the true edge leading, the middle knuckles are to be in the direction of the edge in all cuts and guards, the grip of the handle being held by the thumb and fingers around it.

Prepare for Sword Exercise—Carry the right foot out to the right eighteen inches, the left hand slightly closed a little below the pit of the stomach, being on the same line with the elbow, which will be nearly its height when holding the reins.

Draw Swords—Bring the hand smartly across the body over the bridle arm to the " sword knot," place it upon the wrist, and give the hand a couple of turns inwards, in order to make it fast, and as the handle is grasped, turn the hilt to the rear, and raise the hand the height of the elbow, the arm being close to the body ; by a second motion draw the sword from the scabbard to full extent of the arm, the edge being to the rear, and sink the hand until the hilt is under the chin, the blade perpendicular, the edge to the left, and elbow close to the body, which forms the position of " Recover Swords," then by a third motion bring the hilt down in line with the bridle hand, the elbow near the body, the blade perpendicular, the wrist slightly rounded inwards, which brings it to the position of " Carry Swords."

Slope Swords—Loosen the grasp of the handle, and let the back of the sword fall lightly on the shoulder, the arm remaining in the previous position, but the wrist a little bent upwards.

Right prove distance—Bring the sword to the " Recover ;" by a second motion extend the arm to the right, and lower the sword in a horizontal direction from the shoulder with the edge to the rear, and the shoulders square to the front. " Slope Swords."

Front prove distance—Raise the sword as before; by a second motion extend the arm to the front, and lower the sword in a horizontal direction, edge to the right. " Slope Swords."

Note—Proving distance to the front is only necessary when on foot.

Carry Swords—By a motion of the wrist and fingers resume the grasp of the hand so as to bring the blade upright as before.

Return Swords—Carry the hilt to the hollow of the left shoulder (the blade being kept perpendicular, and the back of the hand to the front), then, by a quick turn of the wrist, drop the point into the scabbard, and resume the first motion in " Draw Swords ;" by a second motion let the sword fall smoothly from the hand, at the same time loosening the sword knot from the wrist ; by a last motion come smartly to the position of " Attention."

Preparatory Instructions in Numbers.

Engage—Carry the sword to the right front, the edge inclining to the right, the point being advanced, and the arm bent, with the back of the hand up, and wrist down ; the sword is then to be carried round in the same position to right rear and passed smartly to left rear by the front, the point down, the " Fort " covering the centre of the body, elbow raised, hand a little lower than the elbow, looking over the arm and sword ; continue this guard to left front, and resume " Right Front Guard."

Assault—Raise the hand and sword to right rear, the arm bent, and edge slightly turned up, the blade over the right shoulder, the body and head turned to the right.

One—Cut horizontally from rear to front at Cavalry, and prepare for Cut " Two," the sword resting on the left shoulder, edge to the front, with elbow raised.

Two—Cut horizontally from front to rear at Cavalry, and prepare for Cut " Three," the arm extended to the rear on a line with the shoulder, the back of the hand turned down.

Three—Cut low from rear to front at Infantry, and prepare for Cut " Four," the back of the sword resting on the left shoulder, point to the rear, shoulders square to the front, and body well bent over.

Four—Cut low from front to rear at Infantry, and prepare for Cut " One " on the left at Cavalry by turning the head and body to the left, sword resting on the right shoulder, hand to the right front, arm bent.

One—Cut horizontally from front to rear at Cavalry, and prepare for Cut " Two," the sword resting on the left shoulder, edge to the rear, hand to the left, elbow raised as high as the shoulder, arm bent.

Two—Cut horizontally from rear to front at Cavalry, and prepare for Cut " Three " at Infantry, arm bent, hand over the right shoulder, sword point downwards, and bend the body over to the left.

Three—Cut low from front to rear, and prepare for Cut "Four," the arm extended to left rear, back of the hand up, edge of the sword down, point downwards to the left rear.

Four—Cut low from rear to front at Infantry, and " Slope Swords."

Note.—If the Recruit fails to carry the edge well in making the " Assault," to attain so essential a requisite for a swordsman, he should be practised in combining the Cuts " One " and " Two " at Cavalry, repeating them several times ; also the Cuts " Three " and " Four " at Infantry.

Right Defend—The hand and elbow well raised to cover the head, the edge of the sword up, the point lowered to the right front.

Second—Carry the hand to the right rear, the sword nearly perpendicular, point up, the " Fort" covering head and neck.

Third—Lower the point to right front, with the edge to the front, the back of the hand to the left, the arm slightly bent, the hand as low as the hip to defend the leg or horse's shoulder.

Fourth—Turn the edge of the sword to the rear, arm slightly bent, as high as in " Third Guard."

Left Defend—Carry the sword by the front smartly to left rear, the " Fort" covering head and neck, point downwards, looking under the arm.

Second—Carry the sword to the left front, the "Fort" covering face and neck, looking under the arm, body square to the front.

Third—Lower the hand to the left rear the height of the hip, point downwards, and edge inclining to the rear, back of the hand kept up, arm slightly bent to defend the leg.

Fourth—Turn the edge of the sword and arm to the front, hand as high as the hip, point downwards, to the left front, arm slightly bent to defend the leg or horse's shoulder.

Slope Swords.

Words of Command.

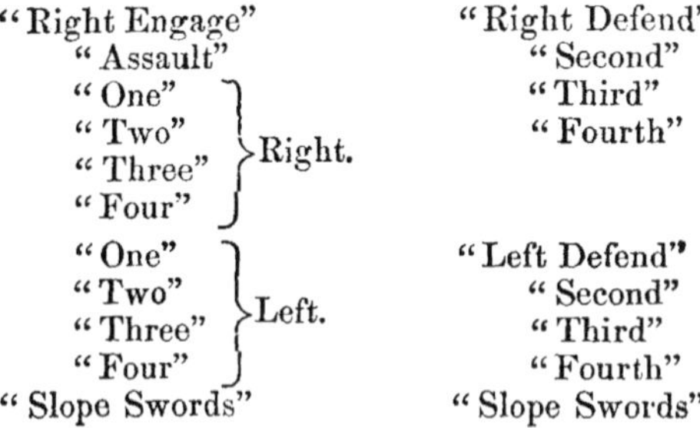

<table>
<tr><td>

"Right Engage"
  "Assault"
    "One"
    "Two"
    "Three" } Right.
    "Four"
    "One"
    "Two"
    "Three" } Left.
    "Four"
"Slope Swords"

</td><td>

"Right Defend"
  "Second"
  "Third"
  "Fourth"

"Left Defend"
  "Second"
  "Third"
  "Fourth"
"Slope Swords"

</td></tr>
</table>

Guards and Points.

Right Defend—Form first guard on the right.

Point—Deliver point with the back of the hand up to the right front at Cavalry, to full extent of the arm, and return to first guard.

Second—Form second guard.

Point—Deliver point at Cavalry, back of the hand up to right rear, and return to second guard.

Third—Form third guard.

Point—Deliver point at Infantry, back of the hand up, to right front, and return to third guard.

Fourth—Form fourth guard.

Point—Deliver point at Infantry, back of the hand up, to right rear, and return to fourth guard.

Left Defend—Form first guard.

Point—Deliver point to left rear at Cavalry, and return to first guard.

Second—Form second guard.

Point—Deliver point to left front at Cavalry, and return to second guard.

Third—Form third guard.

Point—Deliver point to left rear at Infantry, and return to third guard.

Fourth—Form fourth guard.

Point—Deliver point to left front at Infantry, and return to fourth guard.

Slope Swords.

Words of Command.

"Guards" and "Points"

"Right"	"Defend"	"Point"
	"Second"	"Point"
	"Third"	"Point"
	"Fourth"	"Point"
"Left"	"Defend"	"Point"
	"Second"	"Point"
	"Third"	"Point"
	"Fourth"	"Point"

"Slope Swords."

Sword Exercise.

Right Engage—Assault—Prepare for Cut "One" on the right at cavalry.

One—Cut "One," and form first guard.

Point—Deliver point and prepare for Cut "Two."

Two—Cut "Two," and form second guard.

Point—Deliver point and prepare for Cut "Three."

Three—Cut "Three," and form third guard.

Point—Deliver point and prepare for Cut "Four."

Four—Cut " Four," and form fourth guard.

Point—Deliver point and resume fourth guard.

Left Engage—Assault—The same words of command as on the right.

Slope Swords.

Words of Command.

" Sword Exercise"

"Right Engage"	" Left Engage"
" Assault"	" Assault"
"One—Point"	" One—Point"
" Two—Point"	" Two—Point"
" Three—Point"	" Three—Point"
" Four—Point"	" Four—Point"

" Slope Swords."

Pursuing Practice.

Assault—Prepare for Cut " One " on the right front.

One—Make C.. " One " and " Two " in quick succession at Cavalry, and prepare for point to right front, the hand in front of the shoulder, elbow well raised, back of the hand up.

Point—Deliver point to full extent of the arm to right front, immediately turn the back of the hand down, head and body turned to the left front, arm a little bent, point of the sword inclined to the rear for Cut " One " at Cavalry on the left.

One—Make Cuts " One " and " Two " in quick succession at Cavalry, and prepare for point to left front as for right front.

Point.—Deliver point to full extent of the arm to left front, and prepare for Cut " Three " on the right at Infantry.

Three.—Make Cuts " Three " and " Four " on the right in quick succession at Infantry, and prepare to point to the right front, elbow well raised, and hand a little below the shoulder.

Point—Deliver the point to the full extent of the arm, and prepare for Cut " Three " on the left.

Three—Make Cuts " Three " and " Four " in quick succession at Infantry, and prepare to point to the left front as on the right front.

Point—Deliver point to full extent of the arm, and remain steady.

Slope Swords.

Words of Command.

" Pursuing Practice "
" Assault "
" One "—" Point " - - - Right.
" One "—" Point " - - - Left.
" Three "—" Point " - - - Right.
" Three "—" Point " - - - Left.
" Slope Swords."

The men being complete in the Sword Exercise by word of command, will now go regularly through the exercise in the same manner as it will be shown at reviews, inspections, &c., taking the time of each motion (according as Right or Left is attached to the words of command).

Words of Command.

" Right Prove Distance."

" Slope Swords."

" Front Prove Distance."

" Slope Swords."

" Sword Exercise."

" Pursuing Practice."

Section III.

ATTACK AND DEFENCE.

The following practices, with three different modes of Attack and Defence, in four directions, are laid down for independent practice.

Attacking Files.	*Defending Files.*
Right Front.	*Right Front.*

First Practice.   Right Engage.

March—Deliver point and form Fourth Guard; come to Engaging Guard, moving on a horse's length, coming to the Right About, and prepare to Attack on the Left Rear.

Defend by Second Guard and deliver Point; come to the Engaging Guard, and change smartly to Left Rear; prepare to defend.

Second Practice—Cut One and Second Guard, &c., &c.

First Guard, Cut Two, &c.

Third Practice—Cut Two, First Guard, &c.

Second Guard, Cut One, &c.

Left Rear.   *Left Rear.*

First Practice—Deliver Point and form Fourth Guard, moving two horses' length to the Front, and Right About.

Form First Guard, and Deliver Point.

Second Practice—Cut One, First Guard.

First Guard, Cut One.

Third Practice—Cut Two, Second, Guard.

Second Guard, Cut Two.

Change for Left Front Attack, each File taking a side step to his own Right.

Attacking Files.	*Defending Files.*
Left Front.	*Left Front.*

Left Engage.

First Practice—Deliver Point, First Guard ; come to Left Engage, moving on a horse's length, coming to the Left About, and prepare to attack on Right Rear.	First Guard, and Deliver Point; change smartly to Right Rear, and prepare to defend.
Second Practice—Cut One, First Guard, &c., &c.	First Guard, Cut One, &c.
Third Practice—Cut Two, Second Guard, &c.	Second Guard, Cut Two, &c.

Right Rear.	*Right Rear.*
First Practice — Deliver Point, Fourth Guard, moving on two horses' length to the Front, and Left About.	Second Guard, Deliver Point.
Second Practice —Cut One, Second Guard.	First Guard, Cut Two.
Third Practice.—Cut Two, First Guard.	Second Guard, Cut One.

Note.—The same grasp of the sword to be retained throughout the Exercise, to ensure the true Edge leading. All the points are delivered from a defensive position without the fingers relaxing their grasp.

Immediately the Recruit has acquired a knowledge of the exercise, the Squad should be broken into Files, for the purpose of independent play in the practices given with Sticks and Masks.

The Mounted Practice is to be in the same formation as when performing the Practices (already directed) of Attack and Defence ; the Squad being extended, and in two Ranks, they should then go through them at a Canter; and afterwards both Ranks, as in the lesson of the "Double Ride," performing the movements as they pass each other. The opposing Files should also circle "Right" within measure, and at a Walk, before they are allowed to play loose; strict attention being paid that all movements are made from the hips upwards, so as to keep the legs and bridle-arm in their proper position. The loose play, or Independent Practice, having been first tried at a Walk, may be then carried on at a Canter; and the Files should practise on their Left, as well as their Right.

The Cuts and Thrusts must not be given too strongly, as in friendly practice any injury to the parties ought to be avoided.

Each Cut or Thrust to be acknowledged by the party receiving it, by sloping his sword, the Opponent at the same time recovering to an Engaging Guard.

All Cuts or Thrusts being made from a defensive position, great attention should be paid in immediately returning to such, as soon as the Cut or Thrust is delivered.

The practice must never be without Masks; and as the Stick is the substitute for the Sword, the Cut can only be considered fair and effective when given with that part which corresponds with the edge : nor should any movement of attack or defence be attempted with the Stick which could not be performed in a combat with Swords.

It would be useless to endeavour to state which are the best movements, as they must depend entirely upon the judgment and abilities of the parties engaged; but as the loose play should not be allowed until a sufficient competency is attained by the parties, and they have been thoroughly instructed in the movements of Attack and Defence, they can never find themselves at a loss, if the science is followed up by sufficient practice and attention to the instructions they have received.

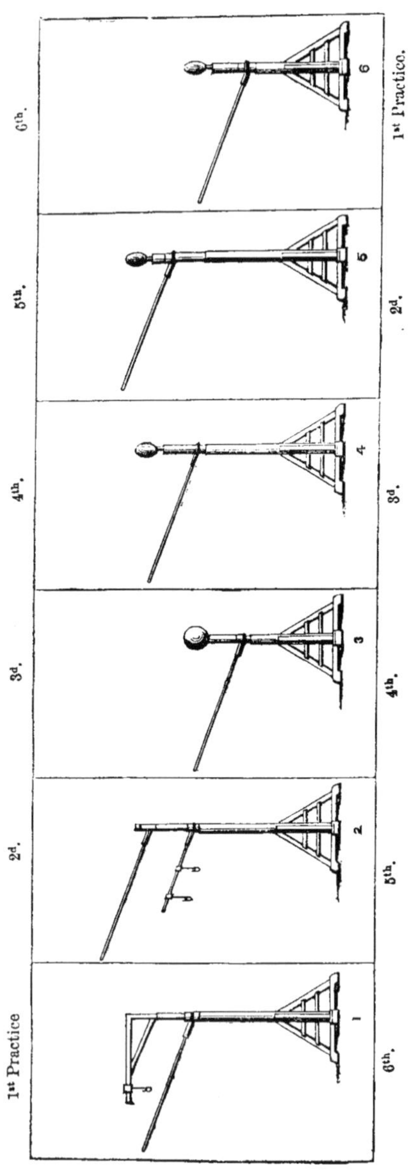

1st Practice
2d.
3d.
4th.
5th.
6th.
1
2
3
4
5
6
1st Practice.
2d.
3d.
4th.
5th.
6th.

Section IV.

POST PRACTICE.

The Squad should now be instructed to Thrust and Cut at the rings and heads attached to the posts, which are supplied to the Cavalry Riding Houses for the practice with Arms. This practice will give a confidence and precision in the application of the Edge and Point, as well as the requisite celerity and judgment of time and measure, as each post having an arm attached to it to represent a sword, lance, or bayonet, the swordsman is consequently forced to turn it out of the line by some mode of defence, before he can make his own offensive movement, both of which must be executed with great quickness; he should therefore be practised, first at a walk, and so on progressively to a canter, &c. It is also requisite that he should be practised to commence with the attack by having the arms of the posts turned outwards, and delivering the Points and the Cuts One, Two, and Three; to do which, in quick succession, the posts are all to be placed on one side of the school. When the school is otherwise occupied this practice may be carried on in the barrack square, or exercising ground, occasionally varying the order of the posts so that a Cut or Point may be alternately given. By placing the posts according to their numbers Four, One, Five, Two, Six, Three, or moving Four, Five, and Six, to the right, the Files passing between the two lines of posts may give the Cuts on the right and Points to the left; it being clearly understood that the movement of attack against each is invariably the same as directed in the Post Practice.

Right Practice.

First   Post, Second Guard, Point.
Second Ditto, Strike the arm forward, Point.
Third Ditto, Fourth Guard, Low Point.
Fourth Ditto, Second Guard, Cut One.
Fifth   Ditto, Strike the arm forward, Cut Two.
Sixth Ditto, Fourth Guard, Cut Three.

The following Left Practice is added, having the posts on the Left, the Files going about, and consequently commencing at the sixth post, which, with the rest, must have the arm turned.

Left Practice.

Sixth   Post, Third Guard, Cut Four.
Fifth   Ditto, Strike the arm forward, Cut One.
Fourth Ditto, First Guard, Cut Two.
Third   Ditto, Third Guard, Low Point.
Second Ditto, Strike the arm forward, Point.
First   Ditto, First Guard, Point.

Note.—In the above practices it will be observed that the Posts No. 2 and No. 5 are those at which the defence is made to the front, whether they are to the Right or Left, and with the remaining four, viz., Nos. 1, 3, 4, 6, it is always made to the Rear.

SECTION V.

GENERAL OBSERVATIONS AND DIRECTIONS.

THE exercise of the Sword consists of Four Cuts or directions of the edge ; the same number of Guards or defensive positions ; and the Point (or Thrust) given with the nails downwards ; therefore, whatever may be the attack or defence, it can only be formed by having recourse to some of the above movements, or a combination of them, as they are all applicable either to Cavalry or Infantry, according to the situation of the parties engaged ; and in all attacks, whether Cuts or Thrusts, the motion ought to increase in speed, the impetus being given at the last.

The greatest attention should at all times be paid to maintain the proper position and balance of the body, from which, by too great an exertion in delivering a Cut or Thrust, the horseman may be suddenly thrown, and thereby lose the advantage of his science in the use of his Sword, by the natural efforts which he must make to regain his seat ;

nor should he fail to have every confidence and dependence upon his Guard, without trusting to his avoiding the attack of an opponent by turning or drawing back the body to escape from it.

In delivering a forward Thrust, very little force is necessary when the horse is in quick motion, as the extension of the arm, with a good direction of the point, will be fully sufficient ; nor should a Cut, under such circumstances, be given too strong, as in both cases the impetus of the horse will give the effective force ; or in the latter, the drawing of the edge can very frequently be applied with advantage, particularly where the Point, by being given too soon, may not have taken effect, when by a quick turn of the wrist the edge is drawn along the face of your opponent, or any part which more immediately comes in contact with it. The forcing also of the edge can be resorted to when very near and closely pressed upon by an adversary, by suddenly extending the arm, and directing the edge across the face, or where an opening is given ; in this case, however, the hand should not be carried more than absolutely requisite either to the Right or Left, or make too wide a movement, so as to offer an equal chance to your opponent.

When sufficient space is allowed for choosing the point of attack, you should endeavour to take advantage of it ; if not, at all events to avoid its being made on your Left rear, when a change of position can alone bring you upon an equality with your opponent : it may be done either by making a sudden halt, so as to allow him to pass, and then pressing upon his Left rear ; or by turning quickly to the Left about, and thereby having your Right also opposed to his. Should you be prevented doingthis, and he still keeps on your Left, you must bear up, as close as possible to him, otherwise your opposition will be ineffectual ; for in his situation, by keeping at the proper distance from you, his Cut will reach when yours will not, and consequently you will be reduced to the defence alone.

In meeting your opponent on the Left front, turn sharply to the left on your own ground, which brings you immediately with your sword-arm free, and at liberty to act upon his left ; and in meeting him upon the Right front, press your horse quickly on, and by a sharp turn to the right, gain his Left rear ; or if pursued, endeavour to keep your

Adversary on the Right rear ; when the distance will be always in your favour, and you may, by the Rear Cut and Point, keep checking his advance with impunity. When attacked by more than one, you will naturally endeavour to keep them both either to the Right or Left ; but where they have been enabled to place themselves on both sides, press close upon the left opponent, and endeavour to keep the right one at a distance.

Although a regular mode is laid down for drawing the sword, yet occasional practice should be given, both on Foot and on Horseback, to come to the "Guard" immediately, and at any required point, without going through the Parade Motions, &c., which will prepare the Swordsman for any sudden attack of an enemy.

The attack or defence against the Lance must depend greatly upon the Rider ; for admitting that the Lancer is equally well-mounted, and skilful in the management of his horse, he will endeavour to keep at such distance as to be out of your reach, whilst he can easily make good his thrust, from the length of his lance ; and he will very frequently succeed in directing his point at your horse, which, becoming unruly, will leave you exposed to the attack of your opponent. You must, therefore, invariably endeavour to gain his Right rear, where he is less able to attack or defend ; whereas if (as against the Sabre) the attack is made upon his Left rear, he has the advantage of resting his lance upon his bridle arm, and can lengthen or shorten his thrust with facility and quickness. If engaged on his Left, the object must be to keep just out of distance of the lance ; watching the opportunity to close, either by having previously formed a defence, or by bearing the lance out of the line. When meeting on his, or your own, Right front, you may have recourse to either of the "Three Practices" (as against the Sword), closing instantly after any of them with confidence and resolution ; he will not then attempt to aim at the horse, as he becomes exposed to any Cut or Thrust, for it is only when engaged directly Right or Left in circling that he gives his short stabs at the horse, without exposing himself, or losing the power of regaining his lance. Your horse should have been well accustomed to the waving of the lance, without which no skill of yours, either in the science of the sword or that of riding, can be of much service to you.

When opposed to Infantry, endeavour to meet an opponent on your Right ; as every Guard parries the point of a sword, so will each defend against the point of a bayonet, taking care that the " Fort" of your own weapon meets the " Feeble" of your opponent's ; consequently it is the bayonet which must be struck ; and supposing the attack to be directed as usual, with the opponent's left shoulder advanced, and on your Right front, the most effectual defence will be as in the Practice against the Posts Nos. 3 and 6, which are similar to the same movements against the sword in the Three Practices of Attack and Defence.

In advancing against Infantry, the Third Guard on the Right or Fourth Guard on the Left leads well to the attack, and is ready for defence, or to take advantage of any opening ; and should your opponent appear irresolute, or draw back his weapon, then, while passing, the Cut Three, or Point, may be given to advantage ; the Cuts Three and Four on the Right or Left, form a defence, as well as an attack, upon Infantry ; and the smarter they are given, the more effectually they will protect you, and cripple your opponent's position. The Point should be used chiefly in pursuit, and will be given with most advantage on your Right, as from thence you can reach further, and are better prepared for defence.

In the use of the sword at speed, there are few things of more importance than that the Horseman should aid the impetus of the Cut, and secure his own seat by supporting the sway of the body with the opposite leg to that side on which he intends to Cut or Point ; for instance, if he desires to cut Three or Four on the near side of the horse, he should support the body by a strong pressure of the inside of the right thigh and leg against the saddle ; *vice versâ* in Cuts made to the right, he should support the body with the left leg ; the lower down the grip can be taken the better, taking care not to touch the horse with the spur at the time of making them. This rule is of greater consequence than it appears to be at first sight ; for unless it is understood and practised, a person may be a very good swordsman, and yet not capable of using his weapon either with effect against an opponent or with safety to himself. It is particularly applicable and necessary in pursuit over rough and varied ground ; and the same observation applies to the use of the Lance.

The instructors should endeavour, as much as possible, in their progressive instructions to the Recruit, to impress upon his mind such occasional observations as become most applicable. Opportunities of thus explaining may often be taking during pauses of rest, as no Squad should be kept too long either in the positions or movements ; and where any Recruits are more deficient than the rest, the whole should be made to cease for the moment, and only those who have gone wrong be required to go on and correct their error.

SECTION VI.

OFFICERS' SALUTE.

OFFICERS fall in Standing at Ease (Close Order), as directed.

Attention—Carry Swords.

Rear Rank take Order—Serrefile Officers come to the front, and place themselves in a line with the Troop leaders in their respective positions.

March—Officers move one pace to thefront.

Present Arms—" Recover Swords," at the second motion of the Carbine, and at the third motion lower the sword (to the full extent of the arm) to the right, with the edge to the left, and point in the direction of the right foot, the arms close to the body.

Advance Arms—" Recover Swords," at the first motion of the Carbine, and at the second motion " Carry Swords."

Rear Rank take Close Order—March—Serrefiles take post in Rear, and Officers step back one pace.

The " Carry Swords," when on Foot, is to be the same as when performing the Sword exercise.

On the March, or when manœuvring, the sword is to be at the slope.

In all Parade movements and on complimentary occasions, mounted, the sword is to be carried with the hilt resting upon the right thigh, the blade perpendicular, the grasp of the lower fingers slightly relaxed.

The Salute on the March is to commence when at ten paces from the Reviewing Officer, taking the time from the Officer on the Right. The sword is then raised, by extending the arm to the right, and by a circular motion brought to the Recover; and continuing the motion to the right shoulder, from whence the sword is lowered, as before directed. The time for completing the Salute on Foot is four paces, commencing with the left foot, and may be divided (for Drill practice) as follows:—First Pace, the sword raised to the right; Second Pace, to the Recover; Third Pace, to the Right shoulder; Fourth Pace, the sword lowered to the right. The same time is given for the Salute when mounted, but the sword should then be kept in a line with the knee. On the March, the above four motions are slowly combined into one graceful move ment.

The head should be slightly turned towards the Reviewing Officer whilst passing him, and having done so six paces, "Recover Swords," at one pace, and " Carry " in the following.

Note.—The Instructions for Foot Parade of Regiment in Cavalry Regulations must be altered to correspond with the above.

SECTION VII.

FORMATION FOR SWORD EXERCISE ON FOOT.

THE Regiment being formed as for Mounted Parade, is told off by squadrons.

From the Right of Squadrons tell off by Fives.

From the Right of Fives to the Front File—The Officers advance two paces, the Right of Fives remain steady, and the remainder face to the right.

Quick March—The whole move forward in succession, keeping their interval and dressing by the Right. The Troop Leaders of the First Squadron raise their Swords and give the base for the alignment. The Rights of Fives of the Front Rank preserve their distance from their Squadron and Troop Leaders; the remainder mark time till each in succession gets his distance of four paces from the man preceding him, particular attention being paid to true covering; Serrefiles and Coverers follow the Lefts of Fives.

Halt.

Prepare for Sword Exercise.

Eyes Right.

Draw Swords.

Slope Swords.

Right Prove Distance.

Slope Swords.

Front Prove Distance.

Slope Swords.

Sword Exercise.

Pursuing Practice.

Front form Ranks.—The Squadron and Troop Leaders turn right about, and move up to the Rights of Fives. The Troops Leaders of the Squadron of Direction raise their swords and give the base.

Quick March—The whole form as at Close Order

Section VIII.

FORMATION FOR SWORD EXERCISE MOUNTED.

From the Right of Threes to the Front File—The Officers in front, and the Rights of Threes, advance one horse's length.

March—The whole move forward in succession by the Squadron of Direction (i.e., the Central Squadron,) taking distance of a horse's length from the head of one horse to the croupe of another ; the Right-hand Man of the Left Troop of each Squadron preserving his former position with respect to the Squadron Leader. The Standards and their Coverers drop back into the Serrefile rank, and all Serrefiles remain in the rear.

Halt—The dressing of the Rights of Threes of the Front Rank, and the covering of the remainder, are corrected as quickly as possible.

Right Prove Distance.

Slope Swords.

Sword Exercise.

Pursuing Practice.

Front form Ranks—Upon the caution, the Standards and their Coverers instantly move to their places.

March—The whole form as at Close Order.

When a regiment, or a portion of it, performs the Sword Exercise Mounted, having advanced from the Right of Threes, it should gallop, and at a signal from the trumpet perform the Sword Exercise ; then turning to the Right About, by a second signal, perform the Pursuing Practice ; then turning the Files again to the Right About, the Line will be formed in the usual manner.

CARBINE EXERCISE.

CARBINE EXERCISE.

CARBINE EXERCISE ON FOOT.

As soon as the Recruit shall have been sufficiently instructed in the Elementary Exercise of Marching, Facing, &c., he is to be taught the Exercise of the Carbine on Foot, and carefully instructed in all the details connected with Loading, Priming, and Firing with Ball, the whole of which are as necessary for the Cavalry as for the Infantry Soldier.

The Exercise of the Carbine on Horseback is to be commenced when the Recruit shall have made a sufficient progress in Horsemanship, as directed in the Instructions on Military Equitation.

Manual Exercise.

The Troop or Squad falls in for Drill, standing at Ease, with Carbine at the " Support ; " that is, with the right hand brought forward and raised, holding the Carbine with the three last fingers under the cock, the thumb above, and the fore fingers under the guard, and about three inches below the bottom of the jacket ; the arms to be kept near the body, the guard of the Carbine turned upwards, the swivel bar touching the hip, and the muzzle to the right rear ; the left hand laid over the right, the left knee bent, and the right foot drawn back six inches.

"*Attention.*" Spring smartly up to the position of the " Advance," that is, with the Carbine perfectly upright against the side, the arm fully extended, the elbow close to the guard of the Carbine to the front ; the thumb above the guard ; the fore finger under it, and the other fingers under the cock.

"*Present Arms.*" The thumb of the right hand is placed under the cock ; the Carbine is raised about two inches, and the muzzle is brought forward from the arm about four inches ; at the same time the left hand is brought briskly across the body and seizes the Carbine a little above the gripe.

"*Two.*" The right hand raises the Carbine, grasping the small of the stock ; the left hand, quitting its position above the gripe, is placed above the lock, fingers round the stock, and the side of the hand resting on the guard ; the point of the thumb as high as, and opposite to, the left eye ; both elbows close.

"*Three.*" The Carbine is brought down to the extent of the right arm, the butt projecting, letting the barrel fall on the bend of the left ; the lock turned a little outwards, and the cock resting against the knuckle joint of the first finger ; this and the second finger only resting on the small of the stock, the others shut in the hand ; the points of the first and middle finger of the left hand touching the swell of the stock in front of the lock, and the first finger close to the middle one, the others shut in the hand ; the point of the thumb touching the seam in the centre of the flap of the trowsers ; the right foot at the same instant drawn back about six inches behind the left heel ; both knees straight.

"*Advance Arms.*" "Advance" the Carbine, steadying it with the fingers of the left hand, and bringing up the right foot.

"*Two.*" Drop the left hand to its place by the side.

"*Port Arms.*" At one motion throw the Carbine to a diagonal position across the body, the lock to be outwards, and at the height of the breast, the right hand grasping the small of the butt, just below the right breast ; the left holding the Carbine at the gripe, the thumbs of both hands pointing towards the muzzle.

N.B. In this position the Carbine may be half-cocked at one motion, by the word "*Half-Cock Arms,*" for the purpose of inspecting the nipple, cock, &c., by placing the thumb of the right hand on the cock, and with the elbow well raised to the front, drawing back the cock to the catch of the half-cock. If the springs are to be eased, at the command "*Ease Springs,*" press the fore finger tightly on the trigger, draw the cock back with the thumb to the full cock, with an equal pressure on the trigger and cock ; then lower it very carefully and gently on the nipple.

"*Advance Arms.*" Bring the Carbine down from the "Port" to the "Advance ; " the left hand steadying it.

"*Two.*" Bring the left hand to its place by the side.

"*Support Arms:*" The right hand is brought forward and raised, retaining its hold of the Carbine as before directed.

"*Stand at Ease.*" The left hand is laid over the right, the left knee bent, and the right foot drawn back six inches.

Platoon Exercise.

"*Spring Arms.*" The Carbine is raised from the "Advance," by the right hand, as high as the hip, with the lock turned downwards, and is seized with the left at the gripe, the right hand seizing the swivel, and securing it through the ring ; then grasp the small of the butt with the right hand.

"*Two.*" Bring the Carbine to the "Advance," and quit it with the left hand.

"*Load.*" Make a quarter face to the right ; drawing the right foot back six inches, bring the left hand smartly across the body ; grasp the Carbine a little above the gripe, and bring it down with the butt against the outside of the left leg and resting on the swivel, the barrel turned towards the front, the muzzle pointed forward and opposite to the middle of the chest, the right hand holding and steadying the muzzle.*

"*Handle Cartridge.*" Carry the hand to the pouch, take hold of a cartridge, draw it out, and bite off the end.

---

* In this position, ramrods are sprung for inspection, or arms examined after firing.

" *Two.*"   Bring the right hand down to the muzzle; shake the powder into the barrel, put in the paper and the ball; and then take hold of the head of the ramrod with the fore finger and thumb.

"*Draw Ramrod.*"   Draw out the ramrod and put it into the barrel, about six inches.

" *Ram Down Cartridge.*"   Push the cartridge to the bottom.

" *Two.*"   Strike it twice smartly with the ramrod.

" *Return Ramrod.*"   Draw the ramrod out of the barrel, and return it into the pipe, forcing it well home; the fore finger and thumb still holding the ramrod.

"*Prime.*"   Bring the Carbine to the " priming position" against the right side, the muzzle raised as high as the upper part of the peak of the chacos or helmet, but pointing directly to the front; the left hand across the body holding the Carbine at the gripe, and the thumb a little above the swivel bar; the thumb of the right hand placed upon the cock, the fingers behind the guard, half-cock the carbine*, and then grasp the small of the butt.

" *Two.*"   Carry the right hand to the cap pocket, take out a cap and place it on the nipple, the thumb pressing on the cap with the fingers shut.

" *Ready.*"   Place the thumb of the right hand upon the cock, the fingers behind the guard; cock the Carbine, and grasp the small of the butt.

" *Present.*"   Raise the Carbine steadily to the " Present," and look along the barrel; place the fore finger before the trigger, but avoid touching it, the Carbine well pressed to the shoulder by the three last fingers of the right hand.

" *Fire.*"   By the action of the fingers alone, and by a gradual but firm pressure, pull the trigger and remain looking along the piece.†

---

* Here remove the old cap if there be one.

† To repeat the practice, at the word " Load " the Carbine may be brought at once from the shoulder to the loading position.

" *Advance Arms.*" Bring the Carbine to the "Advance" and front, bringing the right foot up to the left.

" *Trail Arms.*" Seize the Carbine a little above the gripe with the left hand to steady it, then with the right seize it at the gripe, drop it to the full extent of the arm, and quit it with the left hand, the barrel level, and the muzzle straight to the front.

" *Advance Arms.*" Come to the " Advance."

" *Unspring Arms.*" Raise the Carbine with the right hand as high as the hip, and seize it with the left at the " Gripe," (that is, with the full hand round the barrel and stock,) the lock downwards ; the muzzle raised and in front of the chin ; then " unspring " by disengaging the swivel from the Carbine, drop the swivel behind, and seize the small of the butt with the right hand.

" *Two.*" Bring the Carbine to the Advance and quit it with the left hand.

" *Support Arms.*"   " *Stand at Ease.*"

When the Instructor considers the Squad sufficiently expert in the exercise in slow time by numbers, he will cause it to be performed in quick time without numbers : by the words " *Load,*" " *Ready,*" " *Present,*" " *Fire.*" When fired, come at once to the loading position as before, and the firing is then continued by the words " *Ready,*" " *Present,*" " *Fire.*"

Care must be taken that the distinct motions are not confused by improper haste.

When a certain number of rounds are to be fired, the caution is given, " *Fire* (—) *Rounds, and advance Arms.*"

From the priming position, the firing may be stopped by the words " *Advance Arms.*"

When the Ranks are doubled, the Rear-rank men, at the word " *Load*" or " *Ready,*" take a moderate pace to the right with their right feet, and when the Carbine is brought to the " Advance," resume their former position.

Blank Cartridge Firing.

The Recruit, in loading, is to be instructed to shake the powder well out of the cartridge, and to ram the paper as wadding, home. The Instructor will then make each Recruit fire singly, looking to his levelling, and pay very particular attention that the cheek is not removed, nor must any start of the head be permitted.

When several recruits are steady in their firing singly, they will be placed first in a single rank, that every man may be observed, and two or three men fire together by word of command ; afterwards a couple of files will fire two deep, occasionally changing ranks ; then the files will be increased by degrees, until the Squad fires together.

The Rear-rank men must be particularly attended to, as they generally fire too high ; this is a great fault, and every soldier must be cautioned against it. The lower part of a man's body, at 150 yards, is the best general rule to lay down for aim.

Ball Firing.

The first target for the instruction of Recruits is to be round, and the practice will commence at a distance of thirty yards, so that it will be almost impossible that the Recruit should miss it. This method produces confidence in the young soldier at the commencement of his practice ; for finding that he always hits at a certain distance, he feels encouraged for an increased range.

The range will be increased by degrees to 50—80— 100 yards, at the same target ; when the Recruits separately are steady at these distances, the Instructor will fire them by files, increasing the distance from fifty yards upwards, changing ranks occasionally, and then by the whole Squad.

The Recruit will now practise at a Target of six feet by two, as the last of his drill. This target is divided by black lines into three compartments, Upper, Centre, and Lower divisions, (the centre division having a bull's eye of eight inches diameter in its centre, surrounded, at two inches distance, by a circle of an inch broad,) and is placed at a range of 80 yards, which distance is to be increased as improvement takes place, to 100 and 150 yards.

This division of the target is necessary, in order to correct any soldier's general line of fire, by referring to former practice reports where his shots have been inserted—as, for instance, " always fires low," &c. The Reports must be correctly copied into a book kept by each Troop for the purpose, and signed by the Officer who superintended the practice, according to the following form :

Report of the Target Practice of Capt. . . . . . . Troop, on the . . . Day of								
No.	Name.	Dist. yards.	Hits. Upper.	Hits. Centre.	Hits. Lower.	Total Hits.	Total Misses.	Number of Rounds.	Remarks.
1	Serjeant J. Adam —	100	1	—	2	3	3	6	
2	Corporal B. Brown—	—	—	×1	3	4	2	6	× Outer Circle.
3	Drum. C. Grant —	—	2	o1	—	3	3	6	oBull's Eye.
4	Private A. Alexander	—	—	—	—	—	—	—	In Hospital.
	Total	—	3	2	5	10	8	18	
						(Signed)			J. D., Captain.

USE OF THE CARBINE ON HORSEBACK.

1. When the Recruit has attained a degree of proficiency on foot, the Exercise of the Carbine on Horseback should often form a part of each riding-lesson.

2. The following instructions are given in detail as they are to be taught to Recruits in small Squads; but, as soon as they are perfect, they may proceed with the execution of the several commands without loss of time; and afterwards the Recruit may fire blank cartridge.

3. In the first lessons of the Recruit with the Carbine on horseback great care must be taken, that, in presenting to the front or left, he does not strike or touch the horse's head with the Carbine.

4. In Loading, he must be taught to shake the powder out of the paper into the barrel before he puts in the wadding; and when loading with Ball, to double the Paper round it, so that it may require a small degree of force to drive it home; otherwise, when he " Slings " or " Straps " his Carbine, after it is loaded, the ball is apt to fall out.

5. In priming, the Recruit must be made to understand that the cap when placed on the nipple should be well pressed down with the thumb, so that there may be no danger of its falling off.

6. In all the motions connected with firing, great care must be taken to avoid altering the accustomed feeling of the bridle in the horse's mouth, or the usual seat and balance of the man, and position of his legs, as tending to alarm the animal; for a horse once rendered timid by an accident in firing from his back, will make the practice of it both difficult and dangerous.

7. When the Recruit is familiar with the firings at the halt, he is to practise them while his horse is in

motion ; afterwards he must be taught to fire with ball at a suitable object, first at the halt, and afterwards when in motion. This is the most important part of the instruction ; and it must be recollected that in all Barracks and Quarters near the seaside, there is every facility for firing at a target erected on the shore, without danger or inconvenience.

8. Although it is desirable that the Horseman should be habituated to the use of his Carbine at speed, few occasions can arise for his using it against an enemy at any pace beyond a walk ; and notwithstanding he is enjoined while skirmishing, to keep his horse in motion, in order to avoid becoming a fixed object for the enemy's marksmen, he cannot reasonably calculate on his shot being effective, unless he halts for the moment of firing.

9. The fire of the Cavalry soldier is never to be had recourse to but in skirmishing ; and as the Carbine is only to be used in firing to the front and to the left, the former is generally to be preferred, because in that position the rider has both hands to steady the Carbine, his horse presents the least mark, and he himself is most covered from the shot of the enemy.

CARBINE EXERCISE ON HORSEBACK.

The Squad is to be formed in a rank entire at double open file distance.

"*Spring Arms.*" Take off the right hand glove, place it in the waist-belt; swivel and unstrap the Carbine; and seize the Carbine with the right hand at the gripe.

"*Two.*" Draw the Carbine from the bucket, and continuing to grasp it in the full hand, bring it to the " Advance," resting the hand upon the thigh; the barrel diagonally across the body, the muzzle a little elevated to the left front.

In this position the Carbine is carried by small detachments and advanced parties when near the enemy, and by videttes on service, being that from which the soldier most readily prepares to fire, and which occasions the least fatigue.

" *Load.*" Raise the Carbine in front of the face, pass the butt over to the left under the bridle arm, and lower it till it rests on the swivel, taking hold of it with the left hand to steady it in loading, the right hand holding and steadying the muzzle. In this position the bridle hand must not be raised or disturbed.

" *Handle Cartridge.*" Carry the hand to the pouch, take hold of a cartridge, draw it out and bite off the end.

" *Two.*" Bring the right hand down to the muzzle. Shake the powder into the barrel; then put in the paper, or ball, and lay hold of the ramrod with the fore finger and thumb.

"*Draw Ramrod.*"   Draw out the ramrod, and put it into the barrel about six inches.

"*Ram down Cartridge.*"   Push the cartridge to the bottom.

"*Two.*"   Strike it twice smartly with the ramrod.

"*Return Ramrod.*"   Draw the ramrod out of the barrel, and return it into the pipe, forcing it well home, the fore finger and thumb still holding the end of the ramrod.

"*Prime.*"   Change the right hand to the gripe (below the left) and raise the Carbine, keeping the muzzle well to the front, letting go the left, and continuing to raise the piece with the right till you can pass the butt over to the off side ; lay the Carbine in the left hand, and half-cock.*   Then grasp the small of the butt with the right hand.   This is called the Priming Position.

"*Two.*"   Carry the right hand to the cap pocket ; take out a cap and place it on the nipple, the thumb pressing on the cap with the fingers shut.†

"*Ready.*"   Cock ; then seize the small of the butt with the right hand.

"*Front Present..*"   Raise the Carbine to the "Present" with both hands, and place the butt firmly against the hollow of the right shoulder ; lean the head in order to take a steady aim.   In raising the Carbine to the "Present" the greatest care must be taken not to disturb the feeling of the bridle in the horse's mouth ; and, with this view, the motions must be made as smoothly and quietly as possible ; and, if necessary, the reins may be a little lengthened.

"*Fire.*"   Pull the trigger, still keeping the Carbine at the "Present," and the eye fixed on the object.

"*Load.*"   Lower the butt of the Carbine and bring it down into the loading position.   The remainder of the loading motions as before.

---

* Remove the old cap, if there be one.

† From this position the arms may be advanced if not required to fire.

N.B. Preparatory to firing to the left, the horses must be turned to the right in order to avoid accidents.

"*Ready.*"   As before.

"*Left Present.*"   Raise the Carbine to the " Present " to the left with the right hand ; and in order to steady it, rest the barrel on the left arm, near the elbow, which for this purpose is to be raised almost as high as the shoulder.

"*Fire.*"   As before.

"*Advance Arms.*"   As before."

N.B. The exercise should next be gone through in quick time, without numbers, as on foot.

From the " Advance " the Carbine may be carried or slung.

"*Carry Arms.*"   Without altering the position and grasp of the right hand, raise the Carbine, and place the butt of it in the hollow of the thigh, where the hand previously rested ; the muzzle to be carried to the front, so as to be in a line, clear of the horse's neck, and leaning rather forward ; the elbow near the side.   In this position the Carbine is carried by the advanced guard in marches of parade.

"*Sling Arms.*"   This position is taken from any of the preceding, by gently dropping the Carbine, with the muzzle downwards, behind the thigh, and leaving it slung or suspended by the swivel only.

From being " Slung," the Carbine may be brought at once to any of the foregoing positions, or may be " Strapped."

"*Strap Arms.*"   Seize the Carbine at the gripe, and lay it in the left hand : then place the muzzle in the bucket ; strap and unspring the Carbine, and drop the swivel ; put on the right hand glove, and let both hands resume their usual position.

CARBINE EXERCISE ON FOOT FOR LOADING AND FIRING SHARP'S BREECH-LOADING CARBINE.

WORDS OF COMMAND.

"*Prepare to Load.*" Make a right-half face by raising the toes and turning upon the heels (left toes to point to the front, the right to the right), and bring the Carbine to a horizontal position at the right side with the flat part of the butt between the body and arm above the elbow; grasping it at the same time with the left hand, the little finger immediately in front of the hinge of the "*guard lever*," thumb between stock and barrel, left arm close to the body; the thumb of the right hand in the comb of cock, fingers under the guard, elbow to the rear.

"*Two.*" Carry the left foot six inches to the front, and half cock the Carbine, *and at the same time advance the fingers of the right hand towards the nipple, and with the fore finger throw off the old cap.*

N.B.—The instructions inserted in italics in the foregoing motion, are unnecessary when Maynard's Primers are used.

"*Three.*" Bring the right hand to the "small" of the butt, and with the first joint of the fore finger, draw back the catch which secures the "*guard lever*," thumb pointing to the muzzle; then seize the "*guard lever*" with the fingers, knuckles towards the ground, thumb pointing to the front.

"*Four.*" Push the "*guard lever*" downwards, which will lower the slider forming the breech, then carry the hand to the pouch, and take up a cartridge, holding the bullet between the fore finger and thumb, the powder-case or tail of cartridge to rest on the fingers.

"*Load.*" Carry the cartridge to the breech, and place it on the hollow there to receive it with the point of the bullet in the hand, into which push it forward with the thumb (knuckles to the front, fingers closed in the hand), leaving the end of cartridge *just* outside, then remove the hand to the *"guard lever,"* thumb and fingers outside, knuckles to the right, arms close to the body.

"*Two.*" Close the breech by moving the *"guard lever"* towards the butt (which cuts off the tail end of the cartridge), and fasten the lever by pushing the catch forward with the fore finger; thumb to be on the stock pointing to the muzzle.

"*Cap.*" Carry the hand to the cap pocket, and take up a *cap* between the fore finger and thumb, the remaining fingers closed in the hand.

"*Two.*" Put the *cap* straight upon the nipple, and press it home with the flat part of the thumb, the fingers to be closed in the hand and against the lock plate.

"*Three.*" Bring the hand to the "small" of the butt, and hold it lightly wtth the fingers behind the "*trigger guard*" or "*guard lever,*" the thumb on the stock pointing to the muzzle.

N.B.—The motions to "*Cap*" will be unnecessary when primers are used.

"*At   yards.   Ready.*" Bring the right hand to the sights, and raise the flap for the distance named, then carry the hand immediately to the "small" of the butt, and with the thumb full-cock the carbine, placing the fingers behind the trigger guard, and the thumb on the stock pointing to the muzzle, and fix the eye on an object in front.

"*Present.*" Bring the carbine up to the shoulder at once (carrying the butt to the front, so as to clear the body in doing so), without moving the left hand from the place at which it grasps the stock when at the position of "*Prepare to load,*" or, stooping the body, or raising the heels off the ground, the carbine resting solidly in the palm of the hand; at the same time raise the right elbow nearly square with, and inclined to, the front of the right shoulder, so as to form a bed for the butt, which press firmly into the shoulder with the left hand, and bring the left arm well under the carbine to form a support; the right hand to hold the small of the butt lightly, with the thumb pointing to the muzzle, which is to be a few inches below the object the right eye is fixed upon, the forefinger along the outside of the trigger guard, the left eye closed.

N.B. As the recruit will not get into the position here detailed without practice and much care, the instructor will frequently command "As you were" (when the carbine is to be brought down to the right side), and point out the defects observed. By this means the recruit will soon be accustomed to get into the position readily, acquire a full command of his carbine with the left hand, which is indispensable, and become habituated to handle it with expertness.

" *Two.*" Place the forefinger round the trigger like a hook, that part of the finger between the first and second joint to rest flat on the trigger, and restrain the breathing.

" *Three.*" Raise the muzzle steadily until the fore sight is brought in a line with the object through the bottom of the notch of the back sight.

"*Four.*" Press the trigger without the least jerk or motion of the hand, or arm, and winking of the eye, until the cork falls upon the nipple, keeping the right eye still firmly fixed upon the object.

" *Five.*" Bring the carbine to a horizontal position at the right side, placing the flat part of butt between the body and the arm above the elbow, and half-cock with the thumb of the right hand, *then advance the fingers towards the nipple, and with the fore finger throw off the old cap,* after which draw back the catch with the first joint of forefinger, thumb pointing to the muzzle, and seize the "*guard lever*" with the fingers, knuckles towards the ground, thumb pointing to the front, pressing it downwards to open the breech, and carry the hand to the pouch, and take up a cartridge.

" *Load.*" As before detailed, and so continue by motions until the recruit is habituated to combine them in regular order.

CARBINE EXERCISE ON HORSEBACK, FOR SHARP'S BREECH‑LOADING CARBINE CARRIED IN A BUCKET.

The Squad is to be formed in a rank entire at double open file distance.

"*Spring Arms.*" Take off the right hand glove, place it in the waist-belt; swivel and unstrap the Carbine, and seize the Carbine with the right hand at the gripe.

"*Two.*" Draw the Carbine from the bucket, and continuing to grasp it in the full hand, bring it to the "Advance," resting the hand upon the thigh ; the barrel diagonally across the body, the muzzle a little elevated to the left front.

In this position the Carbine is carried by small detachments and advanced parties when near the enemy, and by videttes on service, being that from which the soldier most readily prepares to fire, and which occasions the least fatigue.

"*Prepare to load.*" Lay the Carbine in the left hand, diagonally across the body, the little finger immediately in front of the hinge of the guard lever, muzzle elevated as high as the chin to the left front, left arm close to the body ; place the thumb of the right hand on the comb of lock, fingers under the guard, elbow to the rear.

"*Two.*" Half cock the carbine (at the same time advance the fingers of the right hand towards the nipple, and with the fore finger throw off the old cap).

"*Three.*" Bring the right hand to the small of the butt, and with the first joint of the fore finger draw back the catch which secures the guard lever, thumb pointing to the muzzle; then seize the guard lever with the fingers, knuckles towards the ground, thumb pointing to the front.

"*Four.*" Push the guard lever downwards, which will lower the slider forming the breech, then carry the hand to the pouch, and take up a cartridge, holding the bullet between the fore finger and thumb, the powder-case or tail of cartridge to rest on the fingers.

"*Load.*" Carry the cartridge to the breech, and place it on the hollow there to receive it with the point of the bullet in the barrel, into which push it forward with the thumb (knuckles to the front, fingers closed in the hand), leaving the end of cartridge just outside ; then remove the hand to the guard lever, thumb and fingers outside, knuckles to the right, arm close to the body.

"*Two.*" Close the breech by moving the guard lever towards the butt (which cuts off the tail end of the cartridge), and fasten the lever by pushing the catch forward with the fore finger ; thumb to be on the stock pointing to the muzzle.

"*Cap.*" Carry the hand to the cap pocket, and take a cap between the fore finger and thumb, the remaining fingers closed in the hand.

"*Two.*" Put the cap straight upon the nipple, and press it home with the flat part of the thumb; the fingers to be closed in the hand, and against the lock plate.

Note.—From this position the arms may be advanced if not required to fire,

"*Three.*" Bring the hand to the small of the butt, and hold it lightly, with the fingers behind the trigger guard or guard lever ; the thumb on the stock pointing to the muzzle.

N.B.—The motions to "Cap" will be unnecessary when primers are used.

"*At   yards. Ready.*" Bring the right hand to the sights, and raise the flap for the distance named; then carry the hand immediately to the small of the butt, and with the thumb full cock the Carbine, placing the fingers behind the trigger guard, and the thumb on the stock pointing to the muzzle, and fix the eye on an object in front.

"*Front Present.*" Bring the Carbine up to the shoulder at once, without moving the left hand from the place at which it grasps the stock when at the position of "Prepare to load," the Carbine resting solidly in the palm of the hand; at the same time raise the right elbow nearly square with, and inclined to, the front of the right shoulder, so as to form a bed for the butt, which press firmly into the shoulder with the left hand, and bring the left arm well under the Carbine to form a support; the right hand to hold the small of the butt lightly, with the thumb pointing to the muzzle, which is to be a few inches below the object the right eye is fixed upon; the fore-finger along the outside of the trigger guard; the left eye closed.

Note.—In raising the Carbine to the "Present" the greatest care must be taken not to disturb the feeling of the bridle in the horse's mouth; and, with this view, the motions must be made as smoothly and quietly as possible; and, if necessary, the reins may be a little lengthened.

As the Recruit will not get into the position here detailed without practice, and much care, the instructor will frequently command "As you were" (when the Carbine is to be brought down to the loading position), and point out the defects observed. By this means the Recruit will soon be accustomed to get into the position readily, acquire a full command of his Carbine with the left hand, which is indispensable, and become habituated to handle it with expertness.

"*Two.*" Place the forefinger round the trigger like a hook, that part of the finger between the first and second joint to rest flat on the trigger, and restrain the breathing.

"*Three.*" Raise the muzzle steadily, until the fore sight is brought in a line with the object through the bottom of the notch of the back sight.

"*Four.*" Press the trigger without the least jerk or motion of the hand or arm and winking of the eye, until the lock falls upon the nipple, keeping the right eye still firmly fixed upon the object.

"*Five.*" Bring the Carbine to the loading position, and half cock with the thumb of the right hand ; then advance the fingers towards the nipple, and with the fore finger throw off the old cap, after which, draw back the catch with the first joint of forefinger, thumb pointing to the muzzle, and seize the guard lever with the fingers, knuckles towards the ground, thumb pointing to the front, pressing it downwards to open the breech, and carry the hand to the pouch, and take a cartridge.

"Load" as before detailed, and so continue by motions until the Recruit is habituated to combine them in regular order.

Note.—The Carbine may be brought down to the "Advance" after firing.

Preparatory to firing to the left, the horses must be turned to the right in order to avoid accidents.

"*Ready.*"   As before.

"*Left Present.*"   Raise the Carbine to the "Present" to the left with the right hand ; and in order to steady it, rest the barrel on the left arm, near the elbow, which, for this purpose, is to be raised almost as high as the shoulder.

"*Advance Arms.*"   As before.

Note.—The exercise should next be gone through in quick time, without numbers, as on foot.

From the "Advance" the Carbine may be carried or slung.

"*Carry Arms.*"   Without altering the position and grasp of the right hand, raise the Carbine, and place the butt of it in the hollow of the thigh, where the hand previously rested ; the muzzle to be carried to the front, so as to be in a line, clear of the horse's neck, and leaning rather forward, the elbow near the side. In this position the Carbine is carried by the Advance Guar in marches of parade.

"*Sling Arms.*" This position is taken from any of the preceding, by gently dropping the Carbine, with the muzzle downwards, behind the thigh, and leaving it slung or suspended by the swivel only.

From being slung, the Carbine may be brought at once to any of the foregoing positions, or may be strapped.

"*Strap Arms.*" Seize the Carbine at the gripe, and place the muzzle in the bucket ; strap and unspring the Carbine, and drop the swivel; put on the right-hand glove, and let both hands resume their usual position.

PISTOL EXERCISE.

PISTOL EXERCISE.

The Squad, being mounted, is to be formed as for the Carbine Exercise.

"*Draw Pistol.*" "*1st Motion.*" Take off the right hand glove, and push forward the cloak, or draw back the sheepskin and shabraque, according to the equipment, and seize the butt of the Pistol with the right hand under the left arm.

"*2nd Motion.*" Draw the Pistol carefully, and bring it at once to the position in which the sword is "Carried," the muzzle upright, the cock resting in the hollow between the thumb and the hand, the lower fingers relaxed and extended along the butt. This position is called the "Advance."

"*Prime and Load—Ram down Cartridge—Make Ready.*" These several motions are to be made in the same manner as directed for the Carbine.

"*To the Front Present.*" From the left hand raise the Pistol with the right, till the breach be nearly as high as, and in line with, the right eye, with the muzzle lowered to the object ; the hand lightly grasping the butt, the arm a little bent, and without stiffness, in order to keep the Pistol more correctly to its aim, and to avoid the shock of a recoil.

"*Fire—Prime and Load.*" As before directed.

Preparatory to firing to the right, or left, the Squad must turn their horses, as directed in firing to a flank with the Carbine.

"*Make Ready.*" As before.

" *To the Left Present.*"   The Pistol to be carried to the left, and raised and levelled as directed in presenting to the front.

" *Prime and Load.*"   As before.

" *To the Right Present.*"   The Pistol is carried to the right, and is raised and levelled as directed in presenting to the front.

" *Fire—Prime and Load.*"   As before.

" *To the Rear Present.*"   Carry the Pistol as far towards the rear as the body, turned in that direction, will admit; take the aim, and hold the Pistol in the same manner as directed for presenting to the front.

" *Fire,*" *&c.*   As before.

" *Return Pistol.*"   " *1st Motion.*"   Drop the muzzle under the bridle-arm, and place the Pistol carefully in the holster.

" *2nd Motion.*"   Bring the right hand to its position by the thigh.

LANCE EXERCISE.

LANCE EXERCISE.

Instruction with the Lance on Foot.

"*Words of Command.*" THE several motions are explained in the instructions in terms applicable to the mounted practice ; but the whole of the exercise is to be taught on foot before the recruit attempts to perform it on horseback.

The formation for exercise on foot is the same as for the mounted practice, and the mounted position is to be retained throughout the drill, commencing with the "Engage." As the lance is brought under the arm, the right foot is carried eighteen inches to the right, and the bridle hand placed as described in the military equitation. At the command "Carry lance," the right heel is brought to the left, and the left hand to the side.

"*Carry Lance.*" The lance is to rest near the man's foot, the right hand grasping the pole at the balance, with the guard and his centre knuckles to the front.

"*Order Lance.*" From the "Carry," the right hand is to slide down the pole to the extent of the arm, the thumb remaining next the body, and the fingers on the outside of the lance.

"*Shoulder Lance.*" The lance is raised about twelve inches from the ground, sloping a little backwards over the right shoulder, the right elbow close to the hip, and the hand below the guard.

"*Support Lance.*" From the "Order," the butt of the lance is raised and brought across the body to the left front, supported at the balance in the right hand, with the thumb outside the pole.

Note.—This position is necessary when the soldier is on sentry with the lance.

Mounting with the Lance.

"*Stand to your Horse.*" The lancer stands square to the front, in line with his horse's fore feet, holding the bridoon rein with the right hand near the bit, and the lance at the "Carry" in the left hand.

"*Prepare to mount.*" As directed in the system of equitation. The lance to be grasped at the balance by the left hand, with the reins and mane.

"*Mount.*" As usual, keeping the point of the lance well up, to prevent it from touching the men or horses near it in the ranks. As soon as the lancer is seated in his saddle, the lance is grasped by the right hand, below the balance under the bridle hand.

"*Two.*" The lance is brought smartly up, and held perpendicular for a moment, with the right hand in front of the face, and the butt of the lance on a line with the elbow ; it is then lowered carefully into the bucket and brought to the position of "Carry lance."

"*Prepare to dismount.*" The right hand slides down the pole of the lance to the extent of the arm.

"*Two.*" The lance is brought smartly up and held perpendicular for a moment ; then lowered under the bridle arm, and grasped at the balance by the left hand, with the reins and mane.

"*Dismount.*" As usual. The hand should press upon the butt end of the pole, and keep the point well raised (to prevent accident) until the lancer "stands to his horse," with the lance at the "Carry" in the left hand.

Dismounting on the "off" side may be often useful, and sometimes even necessary. It should be frequently practised in the riding school, in order to prove the activity of the men, and the steadiness of the horses. It is done by reversing the motion of dismounting. After the man has well secured the lance, reins, and mane in the right hand, the left hand grasps the sword, and lays it across the front of the saddle, the point to the right ; the man dismounts to the "off" side, with the lance at the "Carry" in the right hand.

Mounting on the "off" side is performed by reversing the motions of mounting on the near side.   The lancer must be attentive that he does not entangle himself with his sword, which is passed over behind him, when he is bringing down his left leg into the saddle.

The lance is in all movements to be at the "Carry" or the "Trail," except on the line of march when riding at ease ; it is then to rest in the hollow of the right shoulder, in the position of " Order lance."

The lance may be slung to the right arm for particular purposes, such as leading a horse, firing a pistol, &c., but the sling is strongly recommended to be dispensed with and removed from the weapon on all occasions when the lancer requires to use the lance, as the sling then becomes very inconvenient and has many faults.

" *Carry Lance.*"   The lance is to rest with the butt end in the bucket, and to be kept upright by the right hand, which is to grasp the lance at the balance with the guard to the front.

" *Order Lance.*"   The lance falls against the hollow of the right shoulder, and the right arm extends down the shaft as on foot.

" *Trail Lance.*"   Raise the lance out of the bucket, lower the point to the left front, in the direction of the horse's near ear, the hand resting on the thigh, and the point about twelve inches higher than the man's head.

" *Dressing* "   As usual.   The lance is brought to the position of " Order lance."   As soon as the dressing is ompleted and the command " Eyes front " given, the osition of " Carry lance " is resumed.

Formation for Lance Exercise on Horseback.

" *Form for Lance Exercise.—March.*"   At the command " March," the right of each front rank three of the squadron of direction (*i.e.* central squadron) moves forward, extending from the centre of the squadron, followed by each centre and left of threes.

The rear-rank threes then break off in the same way, the whole extending their front, until each man has an interval of one horse's length from knee to knee, and the same distance from the head of one horse to the croupe of another.

The flank squadrons break off and extend outwards from the squadron of direction, in the same manner and at the same time, at a slight increase of pace, the officers remaining in front, dressing and keeping in line with the base.

"*By Fuglemen.—Lance Exercise.—First Division.—Second Division.* The exercise may be performed at the halt, the walk, or the gallop; if on the move, the "Lance Exercise" is gone through to the front, the "First Division" to the rear (by going files right about), and the "Second Division" to the front (also by files right about).

"*Retreat.—Close to Rallying Distance.*" The files are again put about at the trumpet signal "Retreat," and are closed within two yards of each other at the command "Close to rallying distance."

"*Rally.*" Having retreated to the original or parade line, the ranks are re-formed to the proper front; at the trumpet signal "Rally," officers halt, and take up their alignement, whilst the men turn right about, and form upon them, without hurrying or rushing up confusedly into the ranks.

Each command to be followed by the Trumpet Signal.

"*Front form Squadron.—March.*" Should the exercise be performed at the "halt," the ranks are re-formed by the command "Front form Squadron," "March," or by the trumpet signal "Rally," followed by the word "March." Each man then moves up at a trot into his place, the whole closing their files to the centre of their squadrons.

The intervals of flank squadrons in this case will be unavoidably extended; they are not, however, to be corrected until ordered by the commanding officer.

Note.—If the depth of the front is insufficient for the "Formation for Lance exercise" by advancing and at the same time extending from the squadron of direction, the flank squadrons should first increase their intervals to the breadth of a troop by moving by threes outwards from the squadron of direction ; each squadron can then extend its files from its own centre as it advances, dressing and correcting distance upon the base squadron.

Proving Distance for Lance Exercise at the Halt.

"*Engage.*"   As directed in the "Lance Exercise."

"*Right, prove distance.*"   Carry the point of the lance to the right, turning the body in the same direction.

"*Two.*"   Extend the arm cautiously with the lance, and should the distance be insufficient, "passage" to the left.

"*Three.*"   Withdraw the lance, bringing the hand close to the body.
"Four."   Carry the point of the lance to the "Engage," turning the body to the front.

"*Front, prove distance.*   Extend the arm cautiously with the lance to the front, and should the distance be insufficient "rein back."

"*Two.*"   Withdraw the lance to the "Engage."

"*Carry Lance.*"   Raise the point of the lance, and place the butt in the bucket.

Lance Exercise.

Note.—In performing this exercise the lancer is not to change the grasp of his weapon, but to retain the same hold throughout, as at the "Carry."

"*Engage.*"   Raise the lance out of the bucket and lower the point of it to the front, placing the pole under the right arm, the point on a line with the butt, the hand holding the lance at the balance, and close to the body.

"*Round Wave.*" Move the point of the lance smartly to the left.

"*Two.*" Carry it on the same line to the right.

"*Three.*" Again move it direct to the front.

Note.—The round wave to be made strong and quick, the lance level and firm under the arm, the seat steady in the saddle, moving the body from the hips upwards.

"*First Point.*" Deliver the point with force at the body of the antagonist by extending the arm to the front, raising it on a line with the shoulder, and turning the back of the hand upwards, covered by the guard as a protection from a sword cut; after the point has been delivered, withdraw the lance quickly to the "Engage."

"*Right Front—Second Point.*" Lower the lance and draw it back without altering the grasp, raising the elbow to the rear of the body over the hand, the body leaning forward, and the right shoulder thrown back, the point of the lance directed to the right front.

"*Two.*" Deliver the point with force at the body of the antagonist by extending the arm, raising it on a line with the shoulder, and turning the back of the hand upwards covered by the guard; after the point has been delivered withdraw the lance quickly to the first position.

"*Right, Guard.*" Raise the lance, carrying the point to the left over the head, the butt in a diagonal direction downwards to the right, the arm bent, and hand as high as the shoulder, with the head and body turned in the direction of the guard.

Note.—This guard defends from a sword cut or point on the right side, and may be varied by forming it to the right front or rear; it may also be raised or lowered according to the point of attack. This defence is also applicable to the left and left front.

"*Thrust.*" Raise the lance, extending the arm over the head.

"*Two.*" Strike with the butt at the head of the adversary, leaning the upper part of the body well over to the right to give force to the blow ; then draw back the lance to the first position.

"*Parry.*"   Lower the lance on the right side, holding it perpendicular, with the point over the butt, the hand on a line with and about six inches from the right shoulder, which is to be well thrown back, with the elbow raised and arm bent.

" *Two.*"   By a quick motion carry the lance to the front past the horse's shoulder, parrying forcibly with the butt and then bring the lance back again to the first position.

Note.—This parry is intended to ward off a sword point or bayonet thrust aimed at the right side, and can be also used on the left side.

" *Right Rear—Third Point.*"   Lower the point of the lance to the rear, raising the butt and bringing it over the horse's neck to the left, there placing it across the bridle hand, the right hand turned down close to the body, holding the lance with the guard upwards, and point directed to the right rear, the upper part of the body turned in the same direction.

" *Two.*"   Deliver the point with force at the body of the antagonist by extending the arm, and leaning the body well over, throwing back the right shoulder in doing so ; after the point has been delivered, withdraw the lance quickly to the first position.

" *Left Rear—Fourth Point.*"   Raise the lance over the head, and by a circular motion carry the point by the rear, then lower the lance until it reaches the bridle hand, the point directed to the left rear, the right hand with the elbow well raised about eighteen inches from the left one, the body well turned on the hips to the left rear.

" *Two.*"   Deliver the point with force at the body of the antagonist, by extending the arm and throwing back the left shoulder, and as the arm extends, catch the butt firmly under it close to the body ; after the point has been delivered withdraw the lance quickly to the first position.

"*Left Guard.*" Raise the lance and carry the point by the rear, bringing the butt across the front to the left side, lowering it in a diagonal direction downwards, the arm bent and hand on a line with the forehead.

See note to guard on the right.

"*Thrust.*" Extend the arm upwards to the right, raising the butt as high as the forehead.

"*Two.*" Strike with the butt at the head of the adversary, leaning the upper part of the body well over to the left to give force to the blow ; then draw back the lance to the first position.

"*Left Front—Fourth Point.*" Raise the lance over the head by a circular motion, carry the point by the rear to the left front, then lower it to the position for fourth point.

"*Two.*" As before directed in fourth point.

"*Carry Lance.*" Raise the point, bringing the lance perpendicular on the right side ; the butt is then placed in the bucket.

Words of Command.

Lance Exercise.

	Engage.
Round,	Wave.
	First Point.
Right Front,	Second Point.
Right,	Guard.
	Thrust.
	Parry.
Right Rear,	Third Point.
Left Rear,	Fourth Point.
Left,	Guard.
	Thrust.
Left Front,	Fourth Point.
	Carry Lance.

First Division.

(Cavalry Attack and Defence.)

Note.—It will be observed, in this division, the defence is made immediately after each attack, in order that, should the lancer fail, he may return quickly to a defensive position, from which he is prepared to repeat his attack with thrust or point.

" *Engage.*" Lower the point to the front, and bring the lance under the right arm, as directed in the " Lance Exercise."

" *Right Front, Wave, Second Point, & Guard.*" Carry the point of the lance to the right front.

" *Two.*" Make the " Wave" short and quick to the right and left, about eighteen inches each way, and withdraw the lance for second point.

" *Three.*" Deliver the point to the full extent of the arm and quickly withdraw the lance to the same position.

" *Four.*" Raise the point and form right front guard. —(*See* note to " Right Guard" in " Lance Exercise.")

Note.—The motions of the wave should follow each other in quick succession, as the object is to agitate the flag and cause it to vibrate and thereby alarm the adversary's horse, and also to deceive the opponent as to the precise spot at which the point will be delivered.

In independent practice the wave may be repeated *ad libitum* without stopping between each.

" *Left Front, Wave, Fourth Point, and Guard.*" Lower the lance to the " Engage," with the point to the left front.

" *Two.*" Make the " Wave" left and right, and withdraw the lance for fourth point.

" *Three.*" Deliver the point, and quickly withdraw the lance to the same position.

" *Four.*" Raise the lance and carry the butt over the horse's head, and form " Left Front Guard."—(*See* note to " Right Guard" in " Lance Exercise.")

"*Right Rear, Third Point, and Guard.*" Lower the point of the lance to the right rear, with the back of the hand down for third point.

"*Two.*" Deliver the point to the full extent of the arm, and quickly withdraw the lance.

"*Three.*" By a circular motion carry the point of the lance by the rear, raising it over the head, and lower the butt to right rear guard.

"*Left Rear,*" Fourth Point, and Guard.*" Bring the lance smartly to the position of left rear fourth point.

"*Two.*" Deliver the point to the full extent of the arm.

"*Three.*" Withdraw the lance by raising the hand and elbow, the hand a little above and in advance of the head, the lance point downwards to the left rear.

Note.—This guard is equally effective to the left and left front ; the lancer is also enabled from this guard quickly to return to the attack by lowering his lance for fourth point to any direction on the left, or a point can be made from the guard.

"*Carry Lance.*" Raise the point, bringing the lance perpendicular on the right side ; the butt is then placed in the bucket.

Note.—The attack and defence in this division are equally effective to the right and left.

Words of Command.

First Division.

(Cavalry Attack and Defence.)

Engage.

"Right Front," Wave, Second Point, and Guard.
"Left Front," Wave, Fourth Point, and Guard.
"Right Rear, Third Point, and Guard."
"Left Rear," Fourth Point, and Guard.
Carry Lance.

Second Division.

(Against Infantry.)

" *Engage.*" Lower the point to the front, and bring the lance under the right arm, as directed in the " Lance Exercise."

" *Right Front, First Point, & Thrust.*" Lower the point of the lance to the right front, directing it downwards against infantry.

" *Two.*" Deliver " First Point," and after extending the arm withdraw the lance.

" *Three.*" Raise the point over the left shoulder, extending the arm upwards, and the butt directed downwards for " Thrust."

" *Four.*" Deliver the " Thrust," and after extending the arm as far as the grasp of the lance will admit, withdraw it to the position of " Thrust."

" *Left Front, Fourth Point, & Thrust.*" Lower the point of the lance to the left front for fourth point, directing it against infantry.

" *Two.*" Deliver the " Point," and after extending the arm withdraw the lance for fourth point.

" *Three.*" Raise the point over the left shoulder to the right rear, extending the arm upwards, and the butt directed downwards for " Thrust."

" *Four.*" Deliver the " Thrust, and after extending the arm as far as the grasp of the lance will admit, withdraw it to the position of " Thrust."

" *Right Rear, Third Point.*" Lower the lance, placing it across the bridle hand, the point directed downwards to the right rear for " Third Point."

" *Two.*" Deliver the point to the full extent of the arm, and quickly withdraw the lance for " Third Point."

" *Left Rear, Fourth Point.*" Raise the lance over the head, and by a circular motion carry it to the left rear, with the point directed downwards for fourth point.

"*Two.*" Deliver the "Fourth Point," extending the arm, and quickly withdraw the lance for "Fourth Point."

"*Carry Lance.*" Raise the point, bringing the lance perpendicular on the right side ; the butt is then placed in the bucket.

Note.—The attack in this division is equally effective to the right and left.

WORDS OF COMMAND.

SECOND DIVISION.

(Against Infantry.)

Engage.
Right Front, First Point, and Thrust.
Left Front,   Fourth Point, and Thrust.
Right Rear,   Third Point.
Left Rear,   Fourth Point.
               Carry Lance.

For using the Pistol.

"*Sling Lance.*" From the "Carry" allow the lance to fall back into the hollow of the right shoulder, take off the right-hand glove or gauntlet, place it in the waist-belt, take the sling from the holster pipe, and affix it to the lance within the guard ; sling the lance on the right arm ; the right hand is to rest on the thigh near the hip, and the right arm to be held in a natural position without stiffness.

"*Draw Pistol.*" As directed in the Pistol exercise.

"*Return Pistol.*" As usual.

"*Carry Lance.*" The right hand is to grasp the lance below the guard.

"*Two.*" The lance is brought forward by the right hand sliding up the pole so as to disengage the elbow ; the hand is then reversed and the sling removed, if necessary, and placed in the holster pipe.

OBSERVATIONS.

When ordered to "disperse" in pursuit at field days, the men should be practised to perform the right attack and defence of the first and second divisions, circling their horses at a gallop to the right, and the left attack and defence in circle to the left, taking care that the horses are not galloping false to either hand, and also causing them to "change" at the proper time.

In the attack in line the lances of the front rank are brought to the "Engage" at the command, "The line will attack to the front." It is good practice to make long advances in line with the lances of the front rank at the "Engage," to steady the horses, as they are apt to become excited when the lances are brought down, if only done occasionally in the charge.

After a charge, or attack in line, the lances are raised to the "Carry" at the command, "Halt."

The lancer should be well instructed in the use of his weapon, both in confined situations, as the mêlée, and in the single combat; the heads and posts will afford good practice without the risk of accident, the butt of the lance being used to parry off the wooden arms, and the point to take off the rings and heads. Blunt lances properly balanced would be the best for this practice, until the men are expert, and the horses under perfect control.

A firm seat and light hand are indispensable to the lancer; his horse ought to be stout, active, and well broken, taught to leave the ranks freely, to disperse or attack independently, as in skirmishing, rallying again to any given point at the trumpet signal.

In action the lancer has a decided advantage over those armed with the sword or bayonet, from his greater length of reach and the deadly effect of his lance point; he should, therefore, feel confidence in his weapon and ride boldly at his object.

It will be good practice to let the men attack and defend themselves in circles, as they thereby acquire expertness and power in the use of their weapons and the command over their horses. This manner of attack and defence should be practised with blunt lances and sticks and baskets, both upon the right and left circle.

STANDING GUN DRILL.

STANDING GUN DRILL.

Sec. 1.—*Telling off the Detachments.*

1. THE instructor of the drill should bear in mind, that in every change of numbers at the gun exercise, each recruit has to learn different duties, and to handle different implements from those he was previously engaged with; and these again vary with the several natures of ordnance and machines, all which an artilleryman must be master of; it is therefore impossible that such a variety of exercises can be well executed or even remembered, unless the recruit is made to comprehend the object and motive of the various duties which he is called upon to perform.

2. For the purpose of instructing the recruit, each gun detachment is to be formed in front of the gun, and the different numbers are to be called upon successively to perform their respective duties, while the rest of the detachment look on and observe their motions; and when it is found difficult to make the recruit sensible of the defect of his position, &c., the instructor will place himself, or another recruit in the correct position; the long verbal explanations relative to the disposition of every part of the body and limbs, which drill serjeants usually recite relative to every motion, cannot be retained by the memory of every recruit, and are for the most part a loss of time.

3. Great patience and the utmost precision are necessary on the part of the instructor. He should more especially endeavour to excite a spirited and active deportment in the recruits at every military exercise, and above all be particularly careful not to disgust them by too long an application to any one point in the drill.

4. In the service and exercise of the various descriptions of ordnance, the same numbers, as far as possible, always perform the same duties, the detachments being told off upon the same principle, viz., beginning with the lowest numbers and proceeding to the highest ; No. 1 always commanding.

5. It is presumed that not less than six men (unless from necessity) will be posted to any description of ordnance, except the smaller natures ; when the detachment consists of less than six men, the higher numbers are struck out, and additional duties are imposed on those remaining.

6. The detachment falls in two deep in close order ; the men are so placed that they may be told off to their different duties for which they are most fit. This of course does not apply to the drill of recruits, each of whom must be taught the duties of every number.

7. No. 1 tells them off from the right, No. 2 being the right hand man of the rear rank ; No. 3 the right hand man of the front rank ; No. 4 the second man from the right of the rear ; No. 5 the man in his front, and so on.

Sec. 2.—*Posts of detachment.*

In action.—1. No. 1 at the handspike, Nos. 2, 3 outside the wheels ; with howitzers rather in rear of the muzzle ; with guns in line with the front of the wheels. Nos. 4, 5 in line with the breech, No. 6 five yards in rear of the left wheel, No. 7 in rear of the limber, No. 8 ten yards in rear of No. 6, No. 9 four yards in rear of the limber.

In order of march.—2. No. 1 on the off side at the wheel horses' heads, Nos. 2, 3, in line with the muzzle, Nos. 4, 5 in line with the breech, Nos. 6, 7 in line with the axletree of the limber, Nos. 8, 9 in line with the splinter-bar, the whole at the distance of one yard from the wheels.

In front.—3. In line ten yards in front of the leading horses ; No. 1 on the right of the detachment.

In rear.—4. In line two yards in rear of the muzzle of the gun, No. 1 on the right of the detachment.

Mounted.—5. No. 2 on the left, No. 3 on the right of the gun limber.

With detach- { 4, 12, 1, front rank. { Of which 11 & 12
ments of six. { 7, 11, 6, rear rank. { are horse holders.

With detach- { 4, 12, 5, 1 front rank. { Of which 11, 12,
ments of eight. { 7, 13, 6, 11 rear rank. { and 13 are horse holders.

With detach- { 4, 12, 5, 10, 1 front rank. { Of which 11, 12, 13 are horse holders,
ments of ten. { 7, 13, 6, 14, 11 rear rank. { No. 14 giving his horse to centre driver.

With detach- { 4, 12, 5, 15, 10, 1 front rank. { Of which 10, 11,
ments of twelve. { 7, 13, 6, 16, 11, 4 rear rank. { 12, 13 are horse holders.

At the word "PREPARE TO MOUNT," the men immediately run to their horses, and mount at the word given by the Nos. 1 ; at the word "DISMOUNT," they dismount from the horses and limbers, and take up their places at the gun.

Sec. 3.—*Change of position of detachments when dismounted.*

The detachments being in front.

4, 12, 5, 1.
7, 13, 6, 11.

Change from front to rear.—1. The commanding officer gives "DETACHMENTS REAR," Nos. 1 give *Left about, Wheel, Quick march, Forward, Left about, Wheel, Halt dress.*

Change from rear to front.—2. The commanding officer gives "DETACHMENTS FRONT." Nos. 1 give *Right incline, Quick march, Forward, Left incline, Front, Halt dress.*

Change from right to left.—3. The commanding officer gives " DETACHMENTS LEFT." Nos. 1 give *Right about, Wheel, Quick march, Forward, Right wheel, Right wheel up, Halt dress.*

Change from left to right.—4. The commanding officer gives " DETACHMENTS RIGHT." Nos. 1 give *Lef about, Wheel, Quick march, Forward, Left wheel, Left wheel up, Halt dress.*

Sec. 4.—Detail of duties in the service of ordnance, with detachments of different strengths.

Two men.—No. 1 commands, lays, serves the vent, and fires. No. 2 spunges, loads, and serves ammunition.

Three men.—No. 1 commands, lays, serves the vent, and fires. No. 2 spunges, 3 loads and serves ammunition.

Four men.—No. 1 commands and lays. No. 2 spunges. No. 3 loads and serves ammunition. No. 4 serves the vent and fires.

Five men.—No. 1 commands and lays. No. 2 spunges. No. 3 loads and serves ammunition. No 4 serves the vent. No. 5 fires.

Six men.—No. 1 commands and lays. No. 2 spunges. No. 3 loads. No. 4 serves the vent. No. 5 fires. No. 6 serves ammunition.

Seven men.—No. 7 attends the limber and serves ammunition to No. 6, and occasionally changes with him. The other numbers as before.

Eight men.—No. 8 assists No. 7, and occasionally relieves No. 2. The other numbers as before.

Nine men.—No. 9 attends the ammunition waggon. The other numbers as before.

The drill with diminished numbers should frequently be practised, that each individual may know the duties which he has in that case to perform.

Sec. 5.—*Method of performing the duties of serving ordnance.*

Commanding and laying.—1. No. 1 commands and gives all executive words, whether in action or in movement. He is answerable that all the numbers perform their duties correctly. In action he communicates the directions which he receives from the officer, for the nature of ammunition to be fired, sending No. 7 the length of fuze when firing shells.

2. On giving the word *Load,* he lays his gun sec. 7. When the gun is loaded and layed, he gives the word *Ready,* and steps clear of the wheel to that side where he can best observe the effect of his own shot ; he then gives the word *Fire.* As soon as the gun is fired, he directs it to be run up to its former place, if necessary.

Spunging.—3. Until the word *Load,* No. 2 stands square to his front, in line with the front part of the wheel, holding the spunge about the middle of the staff in his right hand, and trailing it at an angle of 45°. At the word *Load,* he faces to the left, takes an ordinary oblique pace to his right, with his right foot, at the same time brings the spunge smartly to a perpendicular position, by drawing his right hand up in a line with the elbow. The spunge is grasped firmly in the hand, and the rammer head kept just over the right toe ; the elbow close to the side. He next moves his left foot an ordinary oblique pace to his left, bringing the spunge at the same time across his body to the left, so that the right hand may be opposite the middle of it ; he then takes a side step to the right of thirty inches, and bending the right knee brings the spunge to a horizontal position, extending the hands to the end of the staff, the spunge head to the left, the back of the right hand upwards, and that of the left under the spunge head against the side of the muzzle of the gun. He next inserts the spunge head, drops the left hand behind the thigh, shoulders square, straightens the right knee, and bending over the left, forces the spunge home ; he then gives two turns to the spunge, by first lowering his wrist and then raising it, at the same time pressing the spunge against the bottom of the bore ; he next draws out the spunge, at the same time straightening the left knee, and bending over the right, he seizes the staff near the spunge head with the left hand, and places the spunge against the side of the muzzle ; he then turns the spunge, by bringing his hands together in the middle of the staff, and giving it a cant with each hand, and at the same time turning his wrists, which brings the staff horizontal ; he then extends his hands to the ends of the staff, the back of the left being upwards, the other down.

4. If the length of the gun requires it, the spunge is to be pressed home in two motions, No. 2 extending his right hand back to the rammer head as soon as it has reached the muzzle.

5. In spunging howitzers with chambers, No. 2 should press the spunge to the bottom of the chamber, which should be well spunged out ; he wipes the bore by rubbing its whole surface without allowing the spunge to turn in his hand. When he has withdrawn the spunge, he sinks the rammer head till the staff is parallel to the face of the howitzer, which he also wipes clean. Howitzers without chambers are spunged in the same way as guns.

6. At the word *Cease firing*, No. 2 throws the spunge over the axletree of the gun to No. 4, who puts the rammer head into an iron ring at the trail, and afterwards buckles on the spunge head.

Loading.—7. Until the word *Load*, No. 3 stands in the same position as No. 2, upon the word being given, he faces to the right and steps obliquely to his left up to the muzzle of the gun, and then faces again to his right. He brings his hands together to receive the ammunition from No. 6 ; the cartridge in his right, the shot in his left hand. As soon as the spunge is withdrawn, he faces to his left and puts the ammunition into the muzzle (taking care that the seam of the cartridge does not come under the vent), waits till No. 2 has rammed home, and then steps back to his position at the same time that he does.

8. As soon as No. 3 has put in the charge, No. 2 introduces the rammer head into the muzzle, joins his left hand to his right, and rams home, throwing the weight of his body

with the rammer, bending over the left knee, and extending the left arm, back of the hand upwards in a horizontal position over the gun, the hand in line with the shoulder. He next jerks the spunge out with his right hand, allowing the staff to slide through it as far as the middle of it, when he grasps it firmly, and seizes the staff close to the rammer-head, with the left hand, placing it against the side of the muzzle, both knees straight. He then draws his spunge close to his body, and immediately steps back outside the wheel, beginning with his right, then with his left foot so that when the right foot is brought to it, the right hip may be in a line with the front of the wheel; in drawing the right foot to the left, he gives the spunge a cant with his left hand, at the same time quitting it, and brings the spunge to a perpendicular position in the right, the rammer-head resting on the right toe. He remains facing the gun, keeping his eye fixed on the muzzle, and as soon as he sees the flash, he steps in and spunges, &c. as before.

9. If the length of the gun requires it, No. 2 presses home the rammer-head at two motions, as in spunging.

10. With the twenty-four and twelve pounder howitzers, No. 3 puts in the cartridge only, which No. 2 sets home ; No. 3 then puts in the shell, and No. 2 sets it home carefully.

11. With the five-and-a-half inch howitzer, No. 3 puts in the cartridge, receives the shell from No. 8, puts it in, and No. 2 sets it home.

Serving the vent.—12. No. 4 stands in line with the breech, covering No. 2. On the word *Load,* he steps to his left, wipes the vent field with the ball of his thumb, and then places his thumb on the vent, keeping his elbow raised, and his finger on the left side of the gun, so as to allow No. 1 to lay it over his thumb, his right hand on the tube box. When the gun is loaded, he steps to his right, at the same time No. 2 steps back, he uncaps a tube and holds it between the thumb and fore-finger of the right hand, the hand still on the box, and at the word *Ready,* he steps into the gun, pricks the cartridge, drops in the tube, and remains with his left hand over the vent. On the word *Fire,* he steps to his right clear of the wheel. When he sees the flash from the gun he serves the vent as before, at the word *Cease firing,* he receives the spunge from No. 2, as stated in article 6.

Firing.—13. No. 5 stands in line with the breech, covering No. 3. At the word *Load,* he steps to his right, takes the portfirestick out of its socket with the right hand, takes hold of the lighted end of the slow match, from under the apron of the box, and blowing it, lights his portfire; he then steps back to his place, holding the portfire-stick firmly in the right hand (finger nails to the front) outside the wheel, portfire-stick touching it, the portfire inside of it. At the word *Fire,* he raises his hand slowly clear of the wheel, turning the back of the hand to the front, and brings the portfire rather in front of the vent, and fires. As soon as the gun is fired, he lowers the portfire slowly. At the word *Cease firing,* he shifts the portfire into his left hand, cuts it out, and places the stick in the socket. No. 5 is answerable that the slow match is kept burning. If, in firing, the tube blows, No. 1 immediately gives the word *Don't advance,* the tube is blown, upon which No. 3 steps inside the wheel, close to the axletree, No. 4 advances outside the opposite one, and gives the wire to No. 3, who pricks the cartridge; No. 4 then gives him a tube, which he drops into the vent, and they both step to their places.

14. When a lock is used, No. 5 takes the lanyard in his hand, moves to the rear, so far as to keep the lanyard slack, but capable of being stretched without altering his position, which is to be clear of the wheels. When the gun has been fired he coils the lanyard round the bottom.

15. *Firing with the Friction Tube.*— At the word *Load,* No. 5, who is to carry the tube box, takes the lanyard from the trail or button, hooks a tube to it, holding the lanyard in his left hand, the tube in his right; and places himself outside the wheel *facing the breech of the gun,* and looking towards No. 1.

At the word *Ready,* No. 1 raises his right hand above his shoulder with the palm to the front.

No. 4 pricks the cartridge.

No. 5 steps up to the breech of the gun, presses the tube into the vent with the thumb of his right hand, steps back outside the wheel, changes the lanyard from the left to the right hand, and extends it with the hand as high as the vent.

On No. 1 giving the word *Fire*, No. 5 draws the lanyard strongly, but without a jerk, towards his body, on a level with the vent.

As soon as the gun is fired, No. 1 lets his hand fall to his side, and at the command *Cease Firing*, No. 5 hangs the lanyard on the trail or button, and falls into his place.

Serving ammunition.—16. No. 6 stands five yards in rear of, and covering the left wheel. On the word *Load*, he runs back to No. 7, gets a round of ammunition from him, takes the shot in his right, and the cartridge in his left hand, carries them up, and delivers them to No. 3, immediately returns to No. 7 for another, and halts at his own station till the gun is fired. On the word *Cease firing*, he carries the round back to No. 7.

17. With the five-and-a-half inch, and twenty-four pounder howitzer, No. 8 carries up the shell, on the left side, and delivers it to No. 3.

18. With the twelve pounder howitzer, the ammunition is served in the same way as with guns.

19. No. 7 attends at the limber, taking the cartridges from the pouch (which he has placed on the ground) and the shot from the limber box. On the word *Cease firing*, he replaces the pouch in the limber box, and shuts down the lid. When firing shells, he prepares and fixes the fuzes.

20. No. 8 supplies ammunition to No. 6, which he gets from No. 7, holding the cartridge in his right, and the shot in his left had.

21. During the firing, it may be found necessary to run the gun forward, to recover the ground lost by the recoil. At the word *Run the gun forward*, Nos. 2, 3, 4, 5, man the wheels, facing them, and turning them, by means of the spokes. No. 1 heaves at the trail; with heavy guns Nos. 6, 7, assist also at the trail, if necessary. At the word *Halt*, each number returns to his place.

Section 6.—*Ranges.*

1. The range of a piece of ordnance is the distance which the shot passes over from the muzzle, till it reaches the object which it is intended to strike.

Point blank.—2. The point blank range of the shot, is the point at which it would strike when the gun is laid according to sections 7, No. 7, and fired with the service charge.

Line of metal.—3. The line of metal range of the shot, is the point at which it would strike when the gun is laid according to section 7, No. 8, and fired with the service charge.

Extreme range.—4. Is the final spot which a shot reaches.

5. As it is evident that the distance should be known in order to determine whether the gun is to be pointed directly at the object, or above or below it ; artillery-men should be constantly practised in guessing distances, and measuring them afterwards by pacing, until they acquire the habit of estimating them correctly.

6. The following general rules for elevation are easily recollected, and are sufficiently correct, for practice.

Section 7.—*Method of laying a piece of ordnance.*

1. To lay a piece of ordnance, is to place it in such a position that the shot may reach the object which it is intended to strike.

2. For this purpose it is necessary that the eye of the person who lays the gun, and the two notches, one at the top of the base ring, and the other on the swell of the muzzle, be brought into a straight line with the object.

3. That the proper elevation be given to throw the shot the required distance.

Line of direction.—4. The line of direction is taken entirely from the trail, which, by a little practice, can be done with facility and great correctness, the trail being traversed by No. 1 by means of the handspike.

Elevation.—5. This must be given at the breech.

Quarter sight.—6. A scale of quarters of degrees, as far as three degrees, is cut and numbered on the upper quarters of the base ring, beginning from where a horizontal plane passing a little above the axis, on account of the trunnions, would cut it on each side. These divisions are called quarter sights, and by bringing the division expressing the required degree of elevation, and the notch in the side of the muzzle in a line with the object, the gun will have the proper degree of elevation.

Point blank.—7. When the gun is laid by the lowest notch on the base ring, and the notch on the side of the swell of the muzzle, and that these two notches are brought into the plane of the object, the gun is said to be point blank ; thus the gun may be point blank with reference to the object, yet at several degrees of elevation or depression with regard to the horizon.

Line of metal elevation.—8. When the gun is laid so that the notch on the top of the base ring and the notch on the top of the swell of the muzzle coincide with the object, the gun is said to be laid by the line of metal. In this case, in consequence of the dispart, which is half the difference between the diameter of the gun at the base ring and at the swell of the muzzle, the gun will always have some elevation ; this will be greater or less according to the length of the gun, and the difference between the diameters. In general it is about one degree ; any elevation less than this must be given by the quarter sights.

9. Howitzers have a piece of metal cast on the muzzle, which is also called the dispart; so that when the howitzer is laid by the line of metal, it is point blank. This equally applies to guns which have a dispart.

Tangent scale.—10. The tangent scale must be used for all elevations above three degrees, and indeed it is better

to use it whenever the elevation is more than the line of
metal.   It is divided into quarters of degrees, the length of
which depends upon the nature and length of the gun.
When it is used it should be drawn out till the required
elevation appears just at the top of the pipe, when the screw
is turned to fix the scale.   The line of direction is given as
before from the trail, and the elevation from the breech, by
lowering it till the notches in the top of the scale and at
he swell of the muzzle coincide with the object.

11. When great accuracy is required, the line of direction
should be taken at the breech by the line of metal, and
elevation given afterwards.

12. When one wheel stands lower than the other, the gun
will throw the shot out of the direction towards the lowest
side, if it be laid by the line of metal, it should therefore
not be laid directly on the object, but an allowance should
be made, which must be increased in proportion to the
difference of the level of the wheels, and the increase of
range.

Laying.—13. Upon giving the word *Load,* No. 1 takes
hold of the end of the handspike with the right hand, and
of the centre of it with the left, placing his left knee against
his left hand, and bending over it, the right knee slightly
bent, he looks over the top of the gun, and gives the direction.   He then steps up to the breech to give the elevation,
which he does by taking hold of a horn of the elevating
screw, drawing back the right foot, and bending over the
left knee.   When the elevation is given by the quarter
sight, No. 1 places the nail of his thumb in the proper
notch (see No. 6), and raises or lowers the breech according
to the required elevation.   In the drill of recruits No. 1
should be made to name the elevation and range previous to
stepping up to the breech.

Sec. 8.—*Limbering-up.*

1. May be done either to the front, rear, right, or left.

2. No. 1 seizes the handspike and raises the trail, and
carries it round to the right about, Nos. 2, 3 bear down on
the muzzle, Nos. 4, 5 man the wheels.   Nos. 6, 7 assist, if
necessary, No. 1 unships the handspike and buckles it on,

No. 1 will be on the inside of the wheel, at the breech, No. 2 at the opposite side. Nos. 3, 4, 5, in rear of the gun, between the wheels and muzzle on their own side, the limbers come up on the right of the gun, Nos. 2, 3 limber up by lifting at the trail handles, No. 3 keys the gun, No. 1 mounts his detachment.

3. The same numbers perform the duties, but the limber reverses to the left as soon as it arrives at the trail, which is not thrown round.

4. The same as before, but the trail and limber go to the right or left.

Sec. 9.—*Unlimbering, or coming into Action.*

1. May be done either to the front, rear, right, or left, and is the reverse of limbering up.

2. Action front, No. 1 gives the word *Dismount*, No. 3 unkeys the gun, Nos. 2, 3 unlimber, No. 3 gives the words *Limbers march*, Nos. 2, 3 then throw the trail to the left about, Nos. 4, 5 man the wheels, Nos. 6, 7 assist if the nature of the ground requires it; No. 1 unbuckles his handspike and ships it, No. 4 unbuckles the spunge, and gives it over the axletree to No. 2, the whole stand facing to the front till the word *Load* is given.

3. No. 1 is responsible for the correct dressing of his gun when it comes into action.

To the right, left, or rear.—4. The gun is unlimbered by the same numbers, and upon the same principle as in coming into action to the front.

Sec. 10.— *Mounting field ordnance, with the materials belonging to the battery.*

1. When any spars sufficiently long and tackles can be procured, it is best to rig them as sheers, in order to mount the twelve pounder and other heavy guns; this section only applies where such means are not at hand.

2. The medium twelve pounder requires two gun detachments.

3. The light and heavy three pounder, the light six pounder, and the twelve pounder howitzer, are each

mounted by their own detachments ; this may also be done with the heavy six pounder, the nine pounder, the five and a half inch, and the twenty-four pounder howitzer ; but one or two men in addition will greatly facilitate the operation.

4. Nos. 2, 3 attend to the capsquares, and have charge of the muzzle and trunnions ; Nos. 4, 5 attend the cascable and chock the wheels of the light guns, Nos. 6, 7 chock the wheels of the heavy guns, previous to raising the trail No. 1 attends to the elevating screw.

5. The carriages are mounted by their own detachments. With the medium twelve pounder, nine pounder, heavy six pounder, twenty four pounder, and five and a half inch howitzer, Nos. 2, 3, 4, 5, pass a handspike under one of axletrees, and lift one side of the carriage at a time ; Nos. 6, 7, put on the wheels. With the light six pounder, light and heavy three pounder, and twelve pounder howitzer, Nos. 2, 3, in front, Nos. 4, 5, in rear, lift the carriage at once, Nos. 6, 7, each put on a wheel, Nos. 4, 5, attend to the washers and linchpins in both cases.

6. The limbers and waggons are mounted in the same way. The whole detachment assists in lifting the boxes ; after which Nos. 2, 4 lash on the near boxes, Nos. 3, 5, the off-boxes of the limbers, No. 6 the front box, No. 7, the rear box of the waggon body.

First mode.

Medium 12 p.
9 p.
Heavy 6 p.

7. The gun is supposed to be lying vent upwards. A hole is dug close to the muzzle, (about one foot deep for the medium twelve pounder), and sufficiently large to receive the muzzle, the edge of the hole next the gun is cut down to facilitate the entrance of the muzzle ; this will greatly diminish the difficulty of raising the piece, and the trunnions will be at a convenient height for entering the trunnion holes.

8. A handspike is placed at right angles, under the neck of the cascable, and secured there ; it is manned by Nos. 1, 6, 7, 8.

9. Another handspike is placed under the first reinforce ; it is manned by Nos. 2, 3, 4, 5, the two last numbers at the end of it.

10. The middle of the prolonge, or of a piece of a picket rope, or of a drag rope, is fixed by a clovehitch to the neck of the button by Nos. 4, 5 ; it is to be manned by men of the other gun detachment, who, in order to act with greater effect, take hold of it as near the cascable as possible. The carriage is brought close to the gun, leaving room, however, for the men to work.

11. When everything is ready, No. 1 gives the word *Heave*, and as soon as the breech is as high as the mens' hips, Nos. 2, 3, 4, 5, (two at a time,) quit the handspike and man the rope, Nos. 1, 6, 7, 8, must attend carefully to the cascable as the breech is raised. When the piece stands upon its muzzle, Nos. 2, 3, 4, 5, will come up and steady the breech, while Nos. 1, 6, 7, 8, run the carriage within a foot of the gun ; Nos. 6, 7, scotch the wheels, Nos. 1, 6, 7, 8 raise the trail, and when the trunnion holes are opposite to the trunnions, Nos. 2, 3, push the gun over, Nos. 4, 5, bring the rope to the rear, and assist by hawling on it.

12. When the gun does not exactly fall in the trunnion holes, it will probably be between them and the front bolts; in this case the rope is to be passed round under the cheeks, to secure the breech to the carriage ; the trail is then lowered, when the piece will slide into the holes.

13. The nine pounder requires a hole about six inches deep ; a handspike is fixed under the cascable as before ; another handspike under the first reinforce, manned by Nos. 2, 3 ; Nos. 4, 5, at the rope or cascable. The mode of proceeding the same as the medium twelve pounder.

14. The heavy six pounder requires a hole about one and a half foot deep. The mode of proceeding the same as the nine pounder.

Light 6 p.   15. The gun detachment is sufficient ; No. 1
Heavy 3 p. to put the rope through the eye of the cascable; it is manned by Nos. 2, 3, 4, 5, 6.

The carriage is run close to the gun ; at the word *Heave*, the men haul on the rope, and as the breech is raised, Nos. 2, 3, quit the rope to go to the cascable, and steady the gun ; Nos. 1, 6, 7, run the carriage close to the gun ; Nos. 4, 5, heave at the wheels and scotch them. The rope is passed to the rear to Nos. 4 and 5; Nos. 1, 6, 7, raise the trail of the carriage, and when it is high enough, Nos. 4, 5, haul on the rope, and Nos. 2, 3, push the gun into the trunnion holes; the trail is then allowed to come to the ground.

Light 3 p. 16. **No. 1** places a handspike in the bore; Nos. 4, 5, make fast the middle of a lashing rope round the cascable, and the three men can lift the gun on its carriage.

24 p. howitzer. 17. The twenty-four pounder howitzer does not require a hole, a handspike is placed under the neck of the cascable, as with the medium twelve pounder; no handspike is required under the reinforce; Nos. 2, 3, 4, 5, man the cascable rope. (See medium twelve pounder, first mode for the details.)

22 p. howitzer. 18. The howitzer is supposed to be lying in the direction of the trail, the muzzle towards it; a handspike is lashed under the neck of the cascable, manned by Nos. 4, 5, 6, 7, and another is placed under the muzzle, manned by Nos. 2, 3. No. 1 steadies the piece by holding a trunnion in each hand. The howitzer is lifted bodily on the trail till the muzzle is beyond the shoe for the handspike, where it is to rest on the trail; it is then shoved up till the muzzle comes up to the elevating screw, upon the top of which it is to be lifted, the elevating screw having been run up two or three threads, so that the hand-spike may be withdrawn; Nos. 2, 3 shift to the front, taking the handspike with them, put into the bore, and the howitzer is again lifted, and the elevating screw run down as low as possible; the howitzer is then lifted into the trunnion holes.

5½ in. howitzer. 19. The carriage is laid on the ground dismounted, capsquares off, elevating screw screwed down as far as it will go; a shaft under one of the axletrees, the wheels near the points of them; the axis of the howitzer perpendicular to the block trail; a handspike is placed in the bore, manned by Nos. 2, 3, and a shaft over the neck of the button, secured and manned by Nos. 4, 5, 6, 7. No. 1 steadies the piece at the dolphins, at the word *Lift*, the howitzer is lifted on the trail, and slewed round on its reinforce by means of the handspike in the bore, till the axis coincides with the direction of the trail, it is then lifted and shoved forward at four times ; the first till the trunnions touch the brackets ; the second till they touch the rear of the rear eye bolts ; the third between the eye bolts ; and the fourth into the trunnion holes. The cap-squares and elevating screw are adjusted ; the wheels are then put on, as in Section 14, No. 9.

Second Mode.

20. One gun having been mounted by the foregoing mode, the others may be mounted more safely and expeditiously, as follows :—

21. The elevating screw of the gun which has been mounted is not put in, the breech rests upon the carriage, and is lashed to it by Nos. 4, 5. No 6 attaches the pro-longe to the trail. The gun is then run forward towards the muzzle of the dismounted gun, which is lying vent up-wards. Nos. 4, 5, 6, 7, raise the trail of the mounted gun, till its muzzle touches the dolphins of the other, to which it is firmly lashed by a piece of picket rope by Nos. 2, 3. Nos. 4, 5, 6, 7, of the mounted gun, and Nos. 2, 3, 4, 5, of the dismounted gun, haul the trail down to the ground, which lifts the dismounted gun ; this must be done very uniformly, as jerking it is apt to swing the muzzle under the carriage, and jam it under the axletree. Nos. 1, 6, 7, 8, of the dismounted gun, run its carriage forward, so that the wheels of both carriages may overlap, which brings the trunnion holes under the trunnions. These Nos. perform all the duties about the trail of the carriage. The wheels are then scotched, and the trail is raised. The trail of the mounted gun is lifted a little at the same time, which lowers the gun into its place. The wheels of the five and a-half inch howitzer must be sunk at least a foot into the ground, as the gun could not otherwise raise the howitzer sufficiently high to place it on its carriage.

Third Mode.

22. When the ground is soft and can be easily dug, a heavy gun may be mounted, or a gun which has been over-turned bottom upwards, may be righted as follows :

23. An oblong hole, two feet and a half deep, is dug for the muzzle.

24. The gun is supposed to be lying vent downwards ; the wheels of the carriage are scotched, the middle of a

picket rope, or the ends of two drag ropes, are made fast to the trail ; one of them is passed to the front, and manned by Nos. 2, 3, 4, 5 ; the rear one is manned by Nos. 1, 6, 7, 8 ; the trail of the carriage is lifted by the rear men, and hauled over by the others ; Nos. 1, 6, 7, 8, quitting the trail when it is high enough, and holding on upon the rear rope, easing it off gently.

25. The carriage in this reversed position is run over the gun, till the trunnion holes are nearly over the trunnions, a handspike is placed in the bore and manned by Nos. 6, 7 ; and another across it touching the muzzle, and manned by Nos. 1, 8 ; the muzzle is then raised till the trunnions enter the trunnion holes ; Nos. 2, 3, 4, 5, put on the cap squares and key them. If the breech should be so low that the chase touches the breast transom, and prevents the trunnions from lodging in the holes, the breech must first be raised, and a stone or shaft put under it ; when the capsquares are keyed, the breech is lashed to the carriage by Nos. 4, 5, and it is run over the hole. The trail is turned over again as before.

Fourth Mode.

26. When the carriage cannot be righted by the foregoing mode, it may be done by the following. The gun is properly secured as before, one end of the prolonge is passed between the two lower spokes of the wheel which is to be raised, then under the gun and between the lower spokes of the other wheel, it is secured to the nave of it by fastening the rope round the nave, and hooking the hook to the standing part of the rope. The other end of the rope is led up from the lower spokes, rests against the nave of the wheel to be raised, and over the fellies of both wheels ; it is manned by twelve men with twelve pounders, ten with nine pounders, and eight with light guns : four men with heavy, and two men with light guns, stand to the wheel which is to be raised ; two men are posted to the trail, which will make a sweep round horizontally when the carriage is on the point of the axletree, if not attended to. The whole heave together at the word, which throws the weight on the felly of one of the wheels, then on the axletree, and then again on the felly, the pull, therefore, must be steady and uniform, and done as

expeditiously as is consistent with the proper performance of the manœuvre.

27. As a gun may be overturned in the fields and as under such circumstances the gun detachment alone is left with it, which would not be sufficient to haul it over, the prolonge may be attached to the limber hook, and the horses made to draw it. Great care must be taken to stop them in proper time, and to prevent them making any more effort than is absolutely necessary. If the wheel horses are sufficient, the leaders may be unhooked. This mode of righting a carriage, however, shakes the wheel a great deal.

Sec. 11. *Dismounting field ordnance, with the materials belonging to the battery.*

1. Remarks 2, 3, 4, 5 6, Section 10, apply also to this section.

2. Previous to dismounting a gun, the capsquares and handspikes must be taken off, and the elevating screw taken off from the gun.

3. It is to be recollected, that after the gun is disengaged from the carriage, the weight of the trail is much increased, and the men about it should be prepared for this.

Medium 12 pr.   4. A hole a foot deep is dug about a foot from the front of the carriage. The rope is fixed round the neck of the cascable, as in Section 10, No. 10, by Nos. 4, 5; the ends are handed over to Nos. 2, 3, who stretch them out in front; the rope is manned by Nos. 2, 3, 4, 5, and four men of another detachment. Nos. 1, 6, 7, 8, lift the trail. As soon as the muzzle touches the bottom of the whole, the men at the rope haul, and the gun will be disengaged from the carriage. Nos. 2, 3, 4, 5, who are next the gun, come up hand over hand, and steady it ; the carriage is withdrawn, and the gun is allowed to fall on the ground.

Heavy 6 pr. 9 pr.   5. The same as the medium twelve pounder, but one gun detachment is sufficient. The hole for the heavy six pounder must be about one foot and a half deep.

Light 6 pr.
Heavy 3 pr.

6. The rope is fixed round the cascable, as with the medium 12 pounder. Nos. 1, 6, 7, lift the trail ; Nos. 2, 3, haul the rope, and afterwards steady the breech ; Nos. 4, 5, steady the wheels. The carriage is run back by Nos. 1, 6, 7, at the trail, and Nos. 4, 5, at the wheels ; Nos. 2, 3, allow the gun to fall on the ground, vent upwards.

Light 3 pr.

7. Can be dismounted by the same numbers that mounted it, and in the same way.

24pr. howitzer.

8. No hole is required ; it is dismounted in the same manner as the nine pounder, but a drag rope must be fastened to the trail to prevent its flying over, as it must be lifted nearly perpendicularly before the muzzle of the howitzer touches the ground.

12pr. howitzer.

9. Nos. 2, 3, place a handspike in the bore ; Nos. 4, 5, lash another under the neck of the casable ; No. 1 turns the elevating screw as far down as possible. At the word *Lift*, Nos. 2, 3, at the muzzle, Nos. 4, 5, 6, 7, at the breech lift ; and the howitzer is slowly shoved towards the trail, till the muzzle is over the top of the elevating screw ; the muzzle is then lifted, and two or three turns given to the elevating screw, to allow a handspike to pass under the howitzer. Nos. 2, 3, go to the rear, and place their handspike under the neck of the muzzle ; No. 1 stands to the trunnions as in mounting. (Section 10, No. 18.) The muzzle is taken off the top of the elevating screw, and placed on the carriage ; it is then allowed to slide gently down, till it comes to the shoe of the handspike, when it is lifted bodily off, and laid upon the ground. In lifting, the four men at the cascable must not lift too high, or they will throw all the weight on the other two.

5½in. howitzer.

10. The carriage is dismounted by the same numbers, and on the same principle as Section 10, No. 19; care being taken to lower the axletree easily upon the ground. The howitzer is also dismounted on the same principle as it was mounted ; the trunnions resting the first lift between the eye bolts, the second behind the rear ones ; the howitzer must then be allowed to slide down, till the base ring touches the handspike shoe ; it is then slewed round on its reinforce, across the trail, after

which it is lifted bodily off the carriage, and placed upon the ground.

Sec. 12.   *Shifting Shafts.*

1. Suppose the off-shaft to be disabled, and that it is to be replaced by one from the wheel carriage. No. 6 brings up the shaft; No. 3 takes out the linchpin; No. 2 holds up the near shaft as high as necessary; No. 3 disengages the disabled shaft; and No. 6 passes the new shaft through the shaft loop, and holds it till No. 2 fits it on the axletree, and puts it the linchpin. No. 6 takes back the disabled shaft. If not pressed for time, two men are sufficient.

2. To shift the near shaft, No. 3 performs the duties detailed for No. 3, with the off-shaft; and No. 2 those of No. 3; No. 6 as before.

3. The wheel driver may be substituted for one of the gunners; he takes up the new shaft; the leading driver holding his horses.

4. When the wheel carriage is not at hand, one of the waggon shafts must be taken for the gun limber.

5. When the shafts are shifted from double to single draught, and *vice versâ*, the shafts of the gun limber are shifted by Nos. 2, 3, 6, and those of the waggon limber in the same manner by Nos. 4, 5, 7. The off-shaft is shifted first, and then the near one. The wheel driver may hold up the shaft while the other is shifted.

6. A spare shaft may very easily be carried under the body of the waggon.

To drive curricle.

7. The drivers to dismount; the leading driver to remain at his horses' heads; the wheel horses to be disengaged by No. 7, and the wheel driver; Nos. 5, 6 take off the shaft; No. 7 to bear up the near shaft; No. 5 to prepare the sling, and No. 6 the spare handspike; the shaft to be suspended between the wheel horses by the sling; the handspike to be put through the sling, and laid across the saddle and pad of the wheel horses, which are to be driven with reins (made from the Hamburgh line) by the wheel driver, who must

ride on the limbers between Nos. 2, 3 ; the leading driver to remount his horse. During this time the gun can be kept in action, by No. 3 serving himself with ammunition, and No. 4 serving the vent and firing.

Sec. 13. *Disengaging a shaft horse when he falls or is disabled in action.*

1. No. 1 will order Nos. 5, 6, to the rear; No. 11 orders the drivers to dismount and disengage the wheel horse; No. 5 holds the near leader; No. 6 the near wheel horse, and bear up the points of the shaft; No. 7 assists the wheel driver to disengage the wheel horse, leaving the breeching and traces. The off-leader to replace the wheel horse, and No. 6 horse with gunner's harness to replace the off-leader, and when No. 11 sees everything arranged in the rear, is to order Nos. 5, 6, 7, to their gun; which, during this time, is kept in action by No. 3 serving himself with ammunition, and No. 1 pointing and firing.

2. Wheel horses can be substituted for leading horses, by having a loop of rope of 3 feet 8 inches in length, put on to the wheel traces, in the proportion of four per gun or carriage, and one pair of spare per troop.

Sec. 14. *Changing wheels when the lifting jack is not at hand.*

1. A heavy wheel weighs 2 cwt. 13 lbs., a light one, 1 cwt. 3 qrs. ; and each of them requires three men to put it on, and take it off the wheel carriage.

2. The heavy wheel is used for the twelve pounder medium, nine pounder, and heavy six pounder gun ; the twenty-four pounder, and five and a half inch howitzer. The light wheel for the light six pounder and heavy three pounder gun, and the twelve pounder howitzer ; and also for the bodies of ammunition, store and forge waggons, and for all limbers.

3. The wheel carriage of a heavy battery carries a heavy wheel on the axletree arm behind, and one light wheel on each side. A heavy wheel is also carried on the perch of the store waggon. The wheels of the light battery are all the same.

4. In taking the wheels off, and putting them on the wheel carriage, care must be taken to do it gently and firmly, to prevent accidents.

5. To put a wheel on the perch of a waggon, the waggon is unlimbered, and the wheel held upright by one man, with the small end of the nave towards the waggon ; the perch is passed between the two lower spokes, and then allowed to rest on the ground ; the wheel is lifted on the block by two men, and held there till the waggon is limbered up, if there are men enough ; if not, it must be secured to the lashing rings, so as to prevent its falling off. When the waggon has been limbered up, the wheel must be firmly lashed.

6. To take it off the perch, the lashings are loosened, but not so much as to allow the wheel to fall off while the waggon is unlimbering ; as soon as this is done, the lashings are cast off, the wheel lifted off the block, one man keeping it upright, and the waggon is run back from the wheel.

Light 6 pr.
Heavy 3 pr.
12 pr. howitzer.

7. To change the right wheel, Nos. 5, 6, 7 dismount the new wheel ; No. 6 brings it up parallel to the disabled one, and so close to it that it can be taken off without their coming into contact ; No. 1 passes one end of his handspike to No. 2, under the axletree, close to the shoulder, they lift up while Nos. 3, 4 take off the disabled wheel ; Nos. 4, 6 put on the new wheel, and No. 3 runs the other to the rear. If necessary, one end of the drag-rope is made fast to the shoulder of the axletree of the disabled wheel, the other end is passed over the other wheel, and manned by Nos. 5, 7. To change the left wheel, Nos. 1, 3 lift up ; Nos. 2, 5 take off the wheel ; Nos. 4, 6, 7 dismount the new wheel ; No. 6 brings it up ; Nos. 5, 6 put it on ; No. 2 runs the disabled one to the rear ; Nos. 4, 7 man the drag-rope ; Nos. 4, 5 have charge of the linchpins and washers on their respective sides.

8. The men at the handspike must raise the end of the axletree sufficiently high to throw the weight on the other wheel ; and the men who take off the wheel must also lift it, and not increase the weight by allowing it to slide along the axletree.

9. Four men from another gun must man the drag-rope, (*vide* No. 7.) A shaft, manned by Nos. 2, 3, 4, 5, 6, 7, must be substituted for the handspike under the axletree ; Nos. 1, 8 must put on the wheel.

Medium 12 pr.
Heavy 6 pr.
24 pr. } *howitzer*
5¼ in. }

10. The medium twelve pounder wheel may also be changed as follows :—The gun is depressed ; the limber box of the side opposite the wheel to be changed is taken off ; the limber is brought up with its back in front of the gun, the shafts are held up, and it is backed under the muzzle, the wheels of the limber and gun overlapping, the dis· abled wheel being outside ; the muzzle of the gun is to rest nearly on the centre of the axletree ; the wheels of the carriage are scotched ; the men at the shafts bear down, lift the gun, and the wheel is then changed.

11. As the wheels of a light battery are all of the same nature, when the gun wheel is disabled in action, the wheel from the limber may be substituted for it, and the disabled wheel, if quite unserviceable, can be replaced from the wheel carriage or waggon as soon as it can be got up. If the wheel be not quite unserviceable, it may not be put on the limber till a convenient opportunity for exchanging it.

12. The preparations at the gun are the same as before ; when the right wheel of the limber is required to be taken off, the shaft horse to be taken out ; No. 6 takes off the linchpin and washer ; No. 5 to lift by the axletree in rear of the boxes, and No. 7 at the splinter-bar, while No. 6 takes off the wheel.

13. Waggon wheels are changed in the same manner as those of the guns.

Sec. 15. *Shifting the medium twelve pounder.*

1. In performing this operation, the gun is always limbered up, and, if possible, the wheels of the gun and limber should be on a level.

2. When the gun is in the travelling holes, the breech and muzzle are each lashed to the carriage by two lashing ropes, attached to rings in its side. These ropes should be six feet long, with an eye splice at one end. The eye splice is passed through the ring from above, the running end drawn through the eye, and then hauled taut.

3. The gun wheels are scotched by Nos. 2, 3, 4, 5. This precaution, though not always, is sometimes absolutely necessary.

4. The handspike is introduced into the bore ; when the breach is to be raised, the small end is to point upwards ; when the gun is to be lifted, the small end is to point downwards ; No. 5 turns it accordingly.

5. The elevating screw is carried on the side in two iron loops driven into the carriage. The roller is strapped on where the cheek of the carriage joins the block trail. The side arms as usual.

6. When guns are likely to come into action, they should be shifted into the firing holes some time before they arrive at the spot. If they are to debouche and form immediately they should be shifted while under cover. The reverse applies to shifting them into the travelling holes.

Shifting into the firing trunnion holes.

Shift the Gun.—7. No. 1 unbuckles the handspike, and passes it over the nave of the wheel, he takes off the elevating screw, and lays it on the axletree; he then unbuckles the roller, which he keeps in his right hand.

Nos. 2, 3 undo the muzzle lashings, easing off the turns only so much as to allow them to be slipped over the muzzle, and securing the ends by a right draw knot, quite slack. They take off the cap-squares, and then place themselves on each side of the handspike, ready to assist Nos. 4, 5 in lifting the gun. Nos. 4, 5 undo the breech lashings, as directed for those of the muzzle. They go to the muzzle; No. 5 puts the handspike into the bore, point upwards: Nos. 4, 5, place themselves near the end of it, leaving room for Nos. 2, 3 next to the muzzle.

Bear down.—Nos. 4, 5, bear down on the muzzle ; No. 1 places the roller under the first reinforce ring, on the part of the carriage which is marked for it.

Lower.—Nos. 4, 5 lower the breech on the roller ; No. 5 turns the handspike.

Lift.—Nos. 2, 3, 4, 5 lift the muzzle till the trunnions are just clear of the trunnion holes.

Heave.—They step back, No. 1 pushing at the breach till the gun comes to the trunnion holes and falls tnto them ; Nos. 2, 3 put on the capsquares and key them ; No. 5 turns the handspike.

Bear down.—Nos. 4, 5 bear down as far as they can ; No. 1 takes out the roller, and lays it on the trail ; he puts in the elevating screw, and screws it down as far as necessary.

Lower.—Nos. 4, 5, lower the breech gently, that the screw may not be strained ; No. 5 takes out the handspike and passes it over the nave of the wheel ; No. 1 straps on the roller, and also the handspike, unless the gun is to be unlimbered immediately.

When the limber wheels stand lower than the others, considerable exertion is necessary to shift the gun forward.

Shifting into the travelling holes.

Shift the gun.—8. No. 1 unbuckles the handspike and passes it over the nave of the wheel, then unbuckles the roller and lays it on the trail.

Nos. 2, 3 take off the capsquares, and place themselves ready to assist Nos. 4, 5 in lifting the gun.

Nos. 4, 5 go to the muzzle ; No. 5 puts the handspike into the bore, point upwards; Nos. 4, 5 place themselves near the end of it, leaving room for Nos. 2, 3 next to the muzzle.

Bear down.—As before, No. 1 takes out the elevating screw, and lays it on the axletree, and then places the roller under the middle of the first reinforce, up to the cleats on the carriage.

Lower.—As before.

Lift.—As before.

Heave.—Nos. 2, 3, 4, 5 step forward ; Nos. 2, 3 put on the capsquares and key them tight ; No. 5 turns the handspike.

Bear down.—As before, but No. 1 does not put in the elevating screw.

Lower.—As before.

No. 5 withdraws the handspike, and passes it over the nave of the wheel ; Nos. 4, 5 go to the breech ; No. 1 straps on the roller and lodges the elevating screw in its place, and as soon as Nos. 4, 5 have lashed the breech, he straps on the handspike.

Nos. 2, 3, 4, 5 lash the gun at their respective stations in the following manner. Nos. 2, 3 hand the ropes to each other over the chase ; they pass the end of the ropes from above through the rings on their own sides, hauling them as taut as possible ; then they cross the ends over the gun, and secure them on the top by a right draw-knot, which can be easily undone. The breech is secured in a similar manner by Nos. 4, 5, who pass their ropes over the button.

Should the limber wheel stand lower than the others, great attention must be paid not to let the gun slip too quickly to the rear. The gun should only be lifted so high as to keep the trunnions clear of the carriage.

Sec. 16. *Carrying off the gun when the carriage is disabled.*

1. The gun is first dismounted and laid upon the ground. (*Sec.* 11.) The horses are taken out, and the limber is run over the breech of the gun till the hook is over the trunnions ; a handspike is placed in the bore, and the muzzle raised as high as possible, the shafts being lifted at the same time, to bring the gun and hook close together. A picket or drag-rope is passed round the limber hook and the gun in front and rear of both trunnions ; it is then made fast. A box lashing is passed through the loop for the elevating screw, or round the neck of the cascable, and made fast by the midde. As soon as the gun is slung, the shafts are brought to the ground, a man gets on the limber and passes one of the ends of the rope on each side of the near shaft, close to the splinter bar ; the men at the muzzle bear down, and the man at the rope hauls, assisted by another at the side of the limber. When the breech is high enough, the rope is made fast round the shaft by two half hitches ; should there be any doubt as to the strength of the rope, a second one must be applied. The gun when slung must be horizontal.

2. In the mean time the elevating screw and wheels are taken off. (*Section* 11.) The linchpins and washers are

placed in the slow match box; the carriage is then turned bottom upwards, and placed on the limber boxes, with the breast towards the shafts, the axletree nearly over the front of the limber boxes; the proper balance is to be ascertained by lifting the shafts a little up and down, when at the height they generally are when the horses are in the carriage. A picket or drag-rope is passed round the axle-tree, on each side of the cheeks, and round the splinter-bar, the doubling of it frapped together so as to make it tighter, and prevent the carriage slipping back. The wheels outside, undermost, are laid on the top of the carriage, one partly over the other, the upper one being the farthest forward; the balance must be ascertained as before. The wheels are lashed to the part of the axletree arm on which they rest, and to the trail. A piece of rope is then passed round the handspike in the bore and the trail, and hauled taut to steady them. The side arms may be strapped to the box handles or to the gun.

3. As the weight is too much for the limber to travel far, the carriage and wheels may be placed on the body of the waggon as soon as it can be done.

4. The numbers are not told off in this section, as according to the weight of the gun more or less men will be required for each operation. As a general principle, those numbers whose stations at the gun are nearest the work to be performed, will execute it.

Sec. 17. *Exercise with drag ropes.*

1. In the colonies, where there are no horses for the guns, it is necessary to employ men to move them.

2. A light six pounder requires fifteen men, six of whom are told off entirely for the drag-ropes, the other men at the gun assisting also at them, in addition to their other duties. The ammunition must be carried in pouches.

3. The drag-rope men are numbered off from 10 to 15. When the gun is prepared for action, Nos. 10, 12, 14 are with the right drag-rope; Nos. 11, 13, 15 with the left; Nos. 10, 11 carrying the drag-ropes, the hook end in the hand nearest the gun, the remainder of the drag-rope coiled up in the other.

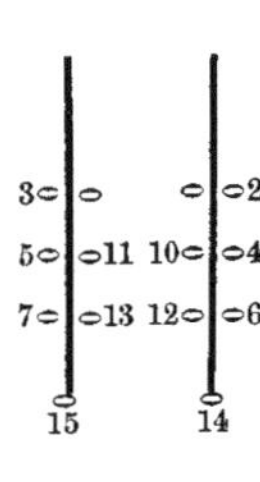

4. At the word "HOOK ON TO ADVANCE," Nos. 10, 11 hook on the drag-washers, turning themselves so as to come inside of the drag-ropes ; Nos. 2, 3 step clear of the drag-rope men ; Nos. 2, 3, 4, 5, 6, 7 move up outside the drag-ropes. Nos. 14, 15 man the loop ends; Nos. 2, 3, 12, 13 the first loops; Nos. 4, 5, 10, 11 the centre loops; and Nos. 6, 7 the rear loops.

5. At the word "ACTION," Nos. 2, 3 step to the right and left, and move to their places ; Nos. 4, 5, 6, 7 fall back to theirs ; Nos. 12, 13, 14, 15 let go the drag-ropes ; Nos. 10, 11 unhook them, and do them up as for action ; the whole fall into their places.

6. At the word "HOOK ON TO RETREAT," Nos. 4, 5 step clear of the drag-rope men ; Nos. 10, 11 hook to the washers, and keep inside of the drag-ropes; Nos. 12, 13, 14, 15 move to the rear inside the drag-ropes ; Nos. 2, 3, 4, 5, 6, 7 move to their places outside the drag-ropes ; Nos. 14, 15 man the loop ends ; Nos. 6, 7, 12, 13 the first loops ; Nos. 4, 5, 10, 11 the centre loops ; and Nos. 2, 3 the rear loops.

7. At the word "ACTION," Nos. 2, 3 step up to the muzzle ; Nos. 4, 5 step to the right and left to allow the drag-rope men to pass them ; Nos. 12, 13, 14, 15 let go the drag-ropes ; Nos. 10, 11 unhook them, and do them up as for action ; and the whole fall into their places.

8. When the detachment is in line, the drag-rope men are on the left ; Nos. 11, 13, 15 in front rank, covered by Nos. 10, 12, 14.

Sec. 18. *Names of the principal parts of a piece of ordnance.*

The length of the gun	Cascable
First reinforce	Bore
Second reinforce	Bottom of the bore
Chase	Mouth of the piece
Muzzle	Axis of the piece

Trunnions
Dolphins
Vent field
Pan
Vent
Swell of the muzzle
Breech
Button
Neck of the cascable
Base ring
First reinforce ring
Second reinforce ring

Shoulder of the trunnions
Diameter of the bore, or calibre of the piece.
Pipe of the tangent scale
Loop for elevating screw
Chamber of the howitzer
Dispart of ditto
Face of the piece
Fillets
Ogees
Astragals

NAMES OF THE PRINCIPAL PARTS OF FIELD CARRIAGES.

Gun Carriage.

Cheeks or brackets
The block or block trail
Trunnion plates, on which the trunnions rest
Trunnion holes
Capsquares
Eye bolts, or capsquare bolts
Keys for capsquares
Axletree (of iron) when in one piece
Axletree arm, when in two pieces
Axletree bed
Breast, or advancing chains
Elevating screw and nut
Handle of the elevating screw
Locking plate
Limbering irons, or handles
Trail plate eye
Handspike ring
Handspike shoe
Handspike pin

Wheel chain, or wheel skid chain
Portfire socket
Side box
Slow match box, with apron and socket
Side arm staples

Limber.

Splinter bar
Swingletree
Trace loops
Stays
Off shaft
Near shaft
Off shaft, wheel iron
Shaft hook. The hook inside of the axletree bed, to which the off shaft is fixed in single draught
Limber hook. In a medium twelve pounder, this is a pintail, and the trail of the carriage is secured to the limber by a chain called the keep or limber chain

Key for limber hook
Shafts
Breeching rings
Shaft staples
Prop
Limber boxes
Guard irons
Box handles
Lashing loop
Tallow box

Waggon Body.

Body
Perch

Side pieces
Battens
Wheel block
Nose plate
Horse shoe boxes

Wheel.

Nave or stock
Nave hoops
Box
Spoke
Felly
Rivets
Tire or streak
Tire or streak bolts

NAMES OF THE DIFFERENT PARTS OF GUNNERS' APPOINTMENTS, SPARE HARNESS, &c.

Bridle.

Bit
Bradoon
Watering
Curb chain
Lip strap
Throat band
Brow band
Reins
Head stall
Collar and chain

Breast Plate.

Rosette and martingale

Saddle.

Tree
Cantle
Flaps
Seat

Pannels
Holster pipes and bear skin flounce
Stirrup leathers and irons
Surcingle
Girth
Crupper
Spareweb harness
Saddle bags
Oil deck.
Cloak
Cloak and baggage straps (3 each)
Sword
Sword knot
Side belt and breast plate
Long and short slings (one of each)
Haversack
Canteen
Forage cord
Nose bag
Corn bag

NAMES OF THE PRINCIPAL PARTS OF THE HARNESS USED IN ARTILLERY.

Near Wheel.	*Near Lead.*
Stirrup leather	The trace
Stirrup iron	Pipe of the trace
Cantle	Galling leather
Pannel	Bridle
Head or pommel	Bridle head or head strap
The breeching	Winker
Join strap	Front
Breeching crank	Cheek
The crupper	Cheek billet
The dock	Throat lash
The collar	Bearing rein with billets
Throat of the collar.	Leading head rein with ditto
The housing	The bit
The hames	Cheek of the bit
Shoulder link and hook	Curb chain
Bottom or breast chain, or link	Mouth piece
Hames strap	Bottom bar
	Snaffle bit
	Head collar
	Nose piece or strap
	Cheek

Off Wheel.

Hand or off saddle
The back band
Shaft tugs
Belly band